Evangelical White Lies

Mike Abendroth

NoCo Media, LLC

ISBN: 978-0-9968198-2-4

Library of Congress Control Number: 2016910221

First Edition

Scripture quotations are from the ESV® Bible (The Holy Bible, English Standard Version®), copyright © 2001 by Crossway, a publishing ministry of Good News Publishers. Used by permission. All rights reserved.

Cover Design: Stephen Melniszyn, Stephen Melniszyn Designs, Tulsa, OK

Internal layout and design: John Manning

"If ever Christians needed to return to the objective, uncorrupted truth of God's Word, it is now. With so many faulty traditions and misinterpretations of Scripture circulating within evangelicalism, Mike Abendroth's book is a timely exhortation that God's Word must be understood and communicated without compromise or defilement. In these last days of widespread deception, there is an urgent need for discernment to identify and reprove the subtle lies that compromise the infallible Word of God. Mike presents a dozen of the most circulated "white lies" within the Christian church, along with the correct interpretation and a clarion call for repentance. His colorful illustrations and passion for the truth coupled with his love for shepherding the sheep have produced a compelling book that will be both instructive and inspiring for those who read it. I highly recommend *Evangelical White Lies* to anyone who desires to protect the glory and honor of our Lord Jesus Christ, the truth of His Word, and the sanctity of His Church."

Evangelist Mike Gendron, Proclaiming the Gospel Ministry

Acknowledgments

...

The unvarnished truth of the matter is this: the Lord has brought so many gifted people into my life, especially when it comes to this project and No Compromise Radio. I am truly a debtor to Christ's mercy. All glory, laud and honor belongs to you, Redeemer King!

Jill Cox and Roger Patterson are skilled editors and have the knack to "see" the manuscript with precision and move it toward clarity. I am thankful they understand NoCo lingo.

John Manning is superb with the keyboard as he lays out the formatting of the book. His guidance in design can only be described with the word, "exactitude."

Stephen Melniszyn is the art guru of all time. I am glad that I will never have to respond to his design work with a "henno!"

Special thanks to John Lawler. His "advice" is spot on and very reliable. I am glad John is on "my side."

The NoCo Radio team is, well, "always biblical, always provocative and always in that order." Especially Tuesday Guy.

Bethlehem Bible Church has blessed me for almost twenty years. I feel sorry for pastors who preach to lesser congregations. SDG!

My family, especially Kim, is, to use 1960s language, both, "groovy" and is as pretty as "a deuce and a quarter." I thank the Lord that her external beauty is only eclipsed by her godliness and desire to exalt Jesus Christ. Hayley, Luke, Maddie and Grace fill my life with wonderful chaos! I love you.

Contents

...

To John MacArthur...

...my father in the faith. May the Lord grant many more men like him to His church, who are lions in the pulpit and kind outside of it.

Foreword

Twenty-one years ago, Janet and I walked into Mike's home in North Hollywood. We were new believers, and I knew we needed to learn the Word of God and to be instructed in sound doctrine. Don't get me wrong, our church was great, but we needed more.

In particular, I needed more. I didn't know why at the time, but I had an insatiable appetite for theology, and Mike's Bible study was an all-you-can-eat buffet. The discussions and debates would continue some nights until way past my bedtime—and this was on a Tuesday night!

Christians, from the newly born to the experienced pastor, have tendencies toward legalism and its opposite, antinomianism. If following Jesus were a road, the road would be noticeably pockmarked by the errors Mike walks through in this book. Every Christian will benefit from reading what he has written. Why? Because he's either made those mistakes or learned to avoid them.

Why are believers prone to wander into these potholes, what Mike calls "white lies," "legends," and "myths"? It's because we want rules. Our hearts long to be told what to do.

Some evangelists like to talk about a "Jesus-shaped hole" in the hearts of unbelievers. Well, that's a white lie of epic proportions. However, believers do have a desire to find a "law-shaped hole" in their hearts.

It's not hard to see why. Being a sacrificial giver takes thought and prayer. Paying a tithe? Easy—and it makes me feel so good because the problem is "solved!" Box checked! God is pleased with me!

Loving God with all my being is hard. Following a checklist of rules I've either made up or learned from someone else? That is perfect! It's also dangerously close to idolatry because now I'm deciding how God should be worshiped and what He demands. It may be well-intentioned, but it's not much more biblically accurate than a Disney character listening to her heart.

At its core, a checklist of dos and don'ts is antithetical to the gospel. Christ delivered us from the Law, so why would we suppose a lesser "law" would be of spiritual benefit?

For some, it is difficult to live a life in light of Isaiah 6: thinking of God's holiness and our utter unworthiness. It's easier to compare ourselves to others—even great men and women of the Bible—because at least they have faults. They sin. We can imagine ourselves "being better" or "almost as good" as they are. I mean, come on, really, how great was Rahab? How great was Samson?

Again, this is faulty reasoning. Christ is the standard. Living a life of gratitude and service is what we are called to, not trying to see if we can reach the level of some biblical hero.

This book calls for the reader to steer clear of the errors that so easily distract us and to keep our focus on Christ. When believers get involved in setting an unbiblical standard of living or thinking, they stray from their calling and disobey their Master.

So, the reader will benefit from the wisdom accrued over more than two decades of full-time ministry. It also reflects years of being steeped in the study of Scripture, theology, and hermeneutics. He's done the hard work, and now you get the benefits. Pretty sweet deal, I think.

Me? Well, I'll mostly think, "I remember this conversation" or "I remember that sermon" or I'll simply be reminded of walking into that first Bible study in North Hollywood and thinking, "You know what? This guy knows something."

Steve Cooley, AKA, "Tuesday Guy"

Introduction and Premise

Liar, liar.

The simple word "liar," repeated twice, opens up a sluicegate of responses and thoughts. And lyrics. Can't you hear Robert Folschow's falsetto vocals as he sings the Dennis Craswell/James Donna, 1965, classic? Try it:

Liar, liar, pants on fire

Your nose is longer than a telephone wire.

If you insist upon Blondie's 1988 cover version, we will allow that.

Is your nose longer than a telephone wire if you only tell white lies? White liar, white liar? The sound is not the same. Not even the Castaway's version played on Gilligan's Island could make that work. White seems pure. Clean. Bare, bald-faced, outright lies seem so, well, nasty. Did you know that barefaced lies originally meant boldfaced lies? The story goes like this: in the 1600s, most men sported facial hair. To have a bare face was bold. Soon, barefaced lie turned into boldfaced lie. Bald-faced must have been the next logical step in the follicle-based discussion. Is it easier to lie through your teeth if you have no hair on your face, or head?

White lies are defined as polite lies. Fibs. Minor. Unimportant. Lies that are tactful. Lies that make the recipient feel good about themselves ("Does this dress make me look good?"). Sometimes white lies make the liar look good ("I did not know that I was speeding, Officer."). Euphemisms cloak inconvenient truths. Diplomacy trumps facts. "But what I said was so well-intentioned!" Altruistic lies? Pants on fire?

Are all lies created equal? Even the ones about Santa Claus? Since God is truth, we must tell the truth. What is the common denominator in the following list?

- Omitting rough edges

- Avoiding uncomfortable facts

- Keeping distress at a distance

- Hiding behind, "We have always taught it like that"

The common theme? These are all things evangelicals do within many of their traditional teachings. Much of modern evangelicalism has its own form of "white lies." Alleged truths that have the feel of truth because they are told and re-told. They "feel" good. They are popular. But they are fibs. They stretch the truth. Web of lies? Maybe that is too extreme. Pack of lies? At least enough for a book. Did you know that the group word for lies is a "pack?"

Does this doctrine make me look theologically fat?

I am not looking to hurt evangelicals with this book. My purpose is to use a "white lie" as a foil to drive you to the Bible and to the person and work of Jesus Christ. Written in a NoCo style (No Compromise Radio's theme is "always biblical, always provocative, always in that order"), the book you are holding is meant to take away any and all theological justifications for the "white lies" found in its chapters. The truth is valuable, even if it makes you look, well, … realistic. (You thought I was going to say "fat.")

Social white lies are often detected by specific verbal and nonverbal signals and traits. Only those with a keen understanding of the Bible and principles of interpretation (hermeneutics) can spot white lies of the evangelical sort.

Resist any and all impulses that make you want to give excuses for unbiblical doctrine, for half-truths, and for falsehoods. While theological white lies often minimize embarrassment, "reduce net harm," and reduce "empathetic distress," they are sinful to the Lord God. Christians have been so influenced by the nurturing, therapeutic culture that they are prone to value relationships at the expense of truth. Don't be "that guy." Don't be "that gal." The perceived value of not wanting to upset the relational apple cart is fleeting. Eventually, truth triumphs. Truth wins. And the sooner you change your mind via repentance and believe the biblical truth, the better. Ask Pinocchio.

We started off this introduction with a musical pop-culture reference, so we might as well end with one. Evangelicalism, can you hide your lying eyes?

Chapter One

. . .

White Lie #1: You Can Live the Gospel

. . .

"It's a boy!"

"Reagan elected in a landslide!"

"Victory for the Allies!"

What do all of these declarations have in common? For many people, these announcements were good news (feel free to substitute "girl," a Democrat, or another victorious country in war if it pleases you). The point remains—each is a publication of good news. There is nothing that must be done. These announcements are not giving any commands. Law is noticeably absent in each statement. Similarly, the gospel is good news about what God has done in the person and work of Jesus Christ, the Savior who triumphed over sin, death, and Satan. Good news.

I want to highlight the importance of the objective declaration of God's good news in Jesus Christ and to stress how every believer is responsible to guarantee its faithful transmission to the next generation. To accomplish this we must believe this good news, protect it, and broadcast it through proclamation (evangelism).

The Legend of Universal Importance

For I delivered to you as *of first importance* what I also received: that Christ died for our sins in accordance with the Scriptures, that he was buried, that he was raised on the third day in accordance with the Scriptures. (1 Corinthians 15:3–4, emphasis added)

Paul knows that the entire Bible is important. He fully grasps the gravity of God breathing out "every jot and tittle" of the Bible (Matthew 5:17–18; 2 Timothy 3:16). Yet, Paul writes "of first importance," meaning that some things are more important than others. Paul acknowledges a hierarchy of biblical truth. Even though every topic and subject in the Bible is important, something is the *most* important.

Before video games ruled the world, boys had to play outside and use their minds to creatively come up with activities. One such pursuit was sneaking grandma's magnifying glass outside on a cloudless, sunny day. Rambunctious boys can readily find the perfect focal point for the sun's rays to be concentrated enough to cause smoke and then fire to belch forth from a dried leaf. But after a while, leaves seem pretty routine and boring. "Been there, burnt that." Then it is time to up the ante to living creatures, namely assorted insects. To continue the analogy, 1 Corinthians 15:3–4 teaches that if all of the Bible was beamed through a magnifying glass, the burning hot focal point would be the substitutionary death, burial, resurrection, and appearance of Jesus Christ.

The Tale of a Passing Fancy

Now I would remind you, brothers, of the gospel I preached to you, which you received, in which you stand, and by which you are being saved, if you hold fast to the word I preached to you—unless you believed in vain. (1 Corinthians 15:1–2)

Paul argues in 1 Corinthians 15:1–2 that it is time to move on from the discussion of worship to the resurrection of the body. Before he lays out the negative and positive ramifications of the resurrection of the body, the apostle reminds them of the gospel that the church heard him preach when he was among them for eighteen months (Acts 18). The Corinthians have already acknowledged the truth of the gospel Paul proclaimed to them. The words "preached" and "received" signify established truth being handed down with the care of passing a baton in a relay. Paul received the good news of God's saving work directly from Jesus Himself (Galatians 1:11), and now Paul was faithful in transmitting the news to the church ("For I delivered to you as of first importance what I also received . . ." 1 Corinthians 15:3). Imagine an Olympic runner refusing the baton from his or her teammate in the final leg of a gold medal relay race. Not Paul.

The church must guard the gospel by protecting it from any system based on works righteousness. The free, sovereign grace of the Triune God mandates watchful custodians who vigilantly "contend for the faith that was once for all delivered to the saints" (Jude 3). Most church members recognize the gravity of guarding the gospel, especially those in leadership positions. There is not much debate here, but the church's weakness shows itself by underestimating the importance of faithfully transmitting the gospel by training the next generation of men and women in the doctrines of Scripture. Listen to Paul charging Timothy to transfer the gospel to one generation of men to the next, so that those men will train others:

> You then, my child, be strengthened by the grace that is in Christ Jesus, and what you have heard from me in the presence of many witnesses entrust to faithful men who will be able to teach others also. (2 Timothy 2:1–2)

There must be a conscious determination to pass the baton to the next generation of Christians. It would be foolish and mythical to believe gospel transmission happens by osmosis. Children need to be taught theology by their parents, and church leaders must instruct the congregations given to their charge. The gospel trust is similar to the stewardship of children; churches, like parents, only "have" them for a short time. Guard the gospel by believing it, protecting it and transmitting it.

The Fable of Friendship Evangelism

The concept of "friendship evangelism" is very popular with this generation. If "friendship evangelism" means that Christians are to be friendly to unbelievers and preach the good news to them, then that is wonderful and should be encouraged. But all too often "friendship evangelism" is a cloak used by people who are too frightened to open their mouths about the exclusivity of Jesus Christ, the only Savior from sin, death, and hell. For them, the focus is upon "friendship" and there is little "evangelism." The Bible does not frown upon preaching the forgiveness of sins to one's friends. God calls believers to proclaim the good news to all people—friends or enemies. Preach to one and to all. Preach to your neighbors and to your children. However, Christians, who can be sinfully prone to be people pleasers, should not attempt to covertly hide behind evangelistic programs touting friendship over faithfulness to God and His Word. Open mouth. Disengage clutch. Preach.

Here is a "hitting the funny bone" moment: it is actually harder to preach Jesus Christ to friends. We feel that if we can establish a friendship with someone, that friendship will serve as the launching pad for discussions about Jesus. Certainly, that can be true and it does occur. But the counterintuitive truth is this: preaching to friends and family is very, very difficult. There are no social mores to consider when I am seated next to a person on a trans-Atlantic flight. They will never see me again. I will never have to celebrate Thanksgiving with them. Christmas eggnog is out of the question. I know there are exceptions, but you know I am generally right. So why are we tricking ourselves with the desire to establish friendships first? My hunch is that we are either afraid or lazy. Or both?

I loved my Grandma and Grandpa Abendroth. Henry and Erna were totally old school. As in, old school Lutherans. German Lutherans. Stoic, German Lutherans. I never remember them talking about God, the Bible, Jesus or church. Except before every meal: "Come Lord Jesus, be our guest, let this food to us be blessed. Amen." Repeat every meal or get scolded. When Grandpa got sick and the doctors warned us that he would not get better, I concocted a strategy to preach the Good News to Grandpa. But that meant getting Erna away from the bedside in the hospital. I knew she would not like me preaching to him. After all, what good is baptismal regeneration? The hatched plot was foolproof. Almost. Kim, my wife, would take Grandma (her real first name was Hedwig) to the hospital cafeteria for lunch and a coffee. I would approach my dear grandfather and proclaim the full forgiveness found in Christ Jesus. I would tell him that he could receive Christ's benefits through faith alone (and not through faith plus infant baptism or any other sacrament).

The second Kim and Erna walked down the hospital corridor I breached the room and sat next to Grandpa. I can hear the exact words that I uttered, even twenty-five years later: "Grandpa, you know how much I love you. If a blindfolded man approached a cliff, and was sure to fall to his death, would it be unkind to tackle him, even if he had the breath knocked out of him? What I am going to say now is going to knock out your proverbial breath. Grandpa, it does not look like you are going to make it. It looks like you are going to die. I am afraid that you are trusting in your religiosity and your baptism for eternal life. If that is the case, when you die, you are not going to heaven—you are going to hell. The Bible says that Jesus Christ, the Savior, perfectly obeyed God's holy laws and He also died on the cross for sinners who broke God's holy laws. He was raised from the dead and is now exalted. You must repent and believe in Him. I am concerned for your soul."

"Nurse." "Nurse!" "NURSE!" Grandma stood at the door yelling. Yelling. YELLING. She knew what I was doing. She did not like it and she screamed for help. Things were never the same between us. I can only hope that the Lord intervened in my grandparents' lives before they died. If I witnessed at the deathbed of someone who was not family, there would be no issues. No breaches in familial love and fellowship. Actually, I have preached to many people on their deathbeds. When I don't know them well, it is so easy to speak about Jesus Christ and His life, death, and resurrection. It is not easy to be at a deathbed, but the words are easy to say. But the second that the person is an unsaved relative or friend, things get super complicated. Friendship makes evangelism harder (usually).

The Fairytale Gospel

When defining terms or concepts it is often helpful to describe the contrast or opposite. Before the definition of the gospel is elucidated, what are some of the definitions of the gospel that are incorrect?

What the gospel is not:

- The Golden Rule
- God helps those who help themselves
- Be good
- Be nice
- Be like Jesus
- The Four Spiritual Laws
- Love the Lord your God
- Love your neighbor
- Repent
- Believe
- Follow
- Have purpose in your life
- Have a relationship with God
- Have your best life now
- Be baptized

- Feed the poor
- Be born again
- Get baptized with the Holy Spirit
- Speak in tongues
- Let Jesus be on the throne of your heart
- Say the "sinner's prayer"
- The fatherhood of God and the brotherhood of man
- Make Jesus your Lord

Many of the above statements are true. After all, some of them are verses from the Bible itself. What is wrong? Exhortations to do something, that is, statements of an imperatival nature, are what theologians call, "law." Law and gospel are mutually exclusive. In addition, the list's common denominator is what is noticeably absent, namely, a declaration of good news, or "the gospel." The gospel says, "This is what God in Christ has done on the behalf of sinners." Law says, "Do this and live."

What is the gospel specifically? Glad you asked.

What Is the Gospel?

> Now I would remind you, brothers, of the gospel I preached to you, which you received, in which you stand, and by which you are being saved, if you hold fast to the word I preached to you—unless you believed in vain. For I delivered to you as of first importance what I also received: that Christ died for our sins in accordance with the Scriptures, that he was buried, that he was raised on the third day in accordance with the Scriptures, and that he appeared to Cephas, then to the twelve. (1 Corinthians 15:1–5)

In 1 Corinthians 15:1–5, Paul reveals six components of the gospel. While there could be more said about the gospel of God elsewhere in Scripture, no other passage contains so much gospel ore found in one mineshaft of truth.

First, the gospel is a declaration. The word "gospel" comes from the Old English, "god-spell," which means "good news." The Greek word signifies "good message." The background of the original words carries military inferences. The general would send a runner to the front of the battle for a report. The runner would hastily return, hopefully with the good news, "We won!" Good news is delivered with what J. Gresham Machen called, "triumphant indicatives,"[1] that is, statements of fact. Therefore, it is wrong to try to "live the gospel." The gospel is good news to be reported, not lived. Michael Horton understands the difference, exclaiming, "Instead of reporting the news, we become the news. In fact, today we often hear Christians speak of 'living the gospel' and 'being the gospel,' as if anything we do and are can be considered a supplement to God's victory in Christ Jesus."[2] Anytime a Christian mixes up the gospel with the law, the gospel evaporates.

Declarations of good news protect God's gospel from any inroads of the law, but pure gospel preaching additionally serves as a built-in protection device from the temptation of the reporter to put his own spin on the story. Heralds of good news should not tell others about themselves, their inner workings, or what they think. Instead, they are to report objective facts. Report! The herald's life is not good news and neither are the felt needs of the hearers. Horton correctly assesses such selfishness, noting:

> We are all "curved in on ourselves." Born with a severe case of spiritual scoliosis, our spines are twisted so that all we can see are our own immediate felt needs, desires, wants, and momentary gratifications. But the gospel makes us stand erect, looking up to God in faith and out to the world and our neighbors in love and service. Not every piece of news can do that, but the gospel can. It is interesting that the biblical writers chose the word "gospel." The heart of most religions is good advice, good techniques, good programs, good ideas, and good support systems. These drive us deeper into ourselves, to find our inner light, inner goodness, inner voice, or inner resources. Nothing new can be found inside of us. . . . The average person thinks that the purpose of religion is to give us a list of rules and techniques or to frame a way of life that helps us to be more loving, forgiving, patient, caring and generous.[3]

---

[1] J. Gresham Machen, *Christianity and Liberalism* (Grand Rapids: Eerdmans, 1923), 39.

[2] Michael Horton, *Christless Christianity* (Grand Rapids: BakerBooks, 2008), 106.

[3] Michael Horton, *The Gospel-Driven Life* (Grand Rapids: BakerBooks, 2009), 20.

True gospel proclamations even guard people from turning personal testimonies into what *they* did, thereby using language like "allowing God to save" them. Testimonies are too man-centered when the announcement of the gospel morphs into "Jesus helped me recover, feel good, and fix my bad relationships." The triumphant, "God saves sinners through the work of Jesus Christ, the risen Savior" must not be tweaked into the law-filled, "be good to others and be a good citizen." News from the eternal God must not be reduced to moralistic ditties and do-dads. I know what a crawdad is but I am not certain about do-dads. Make sure your story of conversion includes what Lorraine Boettner defines this way: "The gospel is the good news about the great salvation purchased by Jesus Christ, by which He reconciled sinful men to a holy God."[4]

Second, the gospel is God centered. The gospel is not good news by announcement only, but it is also good news in the form of content. The subject of almost every verb in 1 Corinthians 15:3–8 is Jesus Christ. To emphasize God's activity in the gospel, Paul even created some passive verbs to keep the stress on God's work ("He was buried," instead of "they buried Him"). God is active and sinners are passive. The Lord is the Savior who does the saving. Faith did not die for sins. Faith was not buried. Faith was not raised and faith did not appear to many after the resurrection. Theologian Sinclair Ferguson understands that you should never put faith in the place of the Savior: "True faith takes its character and quality from its object and not from itself. Faith gets a man out of himself and into Christ. Its strength, therefore, depends on the character of Christ. Even those of us who have weak faith have the same strong Christ as others!"[5]

Should not the church's discussion of Jesus reflect the God centeredness of Scriptures? Dutch theologian Herman Ridderbos knew that Jesus' objective work must take precedence over what happens to a sinner's heart in conversion. Ridderbos said,

> While in Calvin and Luther all the emphasis fell on the redemptive event that took place with Christ's death and resurrection; later, under the influence of pietism, mysticism and moralism, the emphasis shifted to the individual appropriation of the salvation given in Christ and to its

[4]Lorraine Boettner, *What Is the Gospel?* Accessed from http://www.reformed.com/publications/whatisthegospel.php.
[5]Sinclair Ferguson, *The Christian Life* (Carlisle: Banner of Truth, 2013), 67.

mystical and moral effect in the life of the believer. Accordingly, in the history of the interpretation of the epistles of Paul, the center of gravity shifted more and more from the forensic to the pneumatic and ethical aspects of his preaching, and there arose an entirely different conception of the structures that lay at the foundation of Paul's preaching.[6]

Third, the gospel is a historical fact. Jesus lived, died, was buried, was raised, and appeared to others in time on this earth. If Jesus' bones were ever discovered, Christianity would be proven completely false. More than any other religious system, Christianity must include a Jesus who was (and is) a historical figure. Buddhism would survive if Buddha were found to be mythical. Jesus regularly taught in public, was crucified outside of a real city, and could be seen by any and all of the people who lived in Israel two thousand years ago. Paul declared the public and historical nature of Jesus to Festus: "For the king knows about these things, and to him I speak boldly. For I am persuaded that none of these things has escaped his notice, for this has not been done in a corner" (Acts 26:26). Jesus was a real man, although much more than a man, in a real Israel who really died on a real piece of wood at the hands of real Romans.

When the liberal, German theologian Karl Barth came to America to lecture in some universities, then editor for *Christianity Today*, Carl Henry, asked Barth in front of two hundred religious leaders and many news reporters, "The question, Dr. Barth, concerns the historical factuality of the resurrection of Jesus…If these journalists had their present duties in the time of Jesus, was the resurrection of such a nature that covering some aspect of it would have fallen into their area of responsibility? Was it news in the sense that the man in the street understands news?"[7] Henry knew that at the heart of Christianity was the historical nature of the death, burial, and resurrection of Jesus. J. Gresham Machen defended the historical verity of Christianity by boldly asserting,

> From the beginning, the Christian gospel, as indeed the name "gospel" or "good news" implies, consisted in an account of something that had happened. And from the beginning, the meaning of the happening was set forth; and

---

[6]Herman Ridderbos, *Paul: An Outline of His Theology* (Grand Rapids: Wm. B. Eerdmans Publishing Company, 1997), 14.
[7]Carl Henry, *Confessions of a Theologian* (Grand Rapids: Word, 1986), 211.

when the meaning of the happening was set forth then there was Christian doctrine. "Christ died"—that is history; "Christ died for our sins"—that is doctrine. Without these two elements, joined in an absolutely indissoluble union, there is no Christianity. The coming of Jesus was understood now as an act of God by which sinful men were saved. The primitive Church was concerned not merely with what Jesus had said, but also, and primarily, with what Jesus had done. The world was to be redeemed through the proclamation of an event. And with the event went the meaning of the event; and the setting forth of the event with the meaning of the event was doctrine. These two elements are always combined in the Christian message. The narration of the facts is history; the narration of the facts with the meaning of the facts is doctrine. "Suffered under Pontius Pilate, was crucified, dead and buried"—that is history. "He loved me and gave Himself for me"—that is doctrine. Such was the Christianity of the primitive Church.[8]

Fourth, the gospel is doctrinal. Doctrine is any statement of truth about God. In 1 Corinthians 15:3, Paul emphasizes the doctrine of substitutionary atonement with the words, "Christ died for our sins." Paul's language reflects Old Testament passages such as Isaiah 53 where God's Servant, the Shepherd of the people, becomes the sacrifice for them. The atoning death of the sinless Jesus for others is a common and biblical teaching (Romans 5:6–8, 8:32; 1 Corinthians 8:11; 2 Corinthians 5:14–15; Titus 2:14; Galatians 1:4).

Vicarious substitution, or penal substitution, is under attack, even by some professing evangelicals. While Jesus' death was certainly an example of love, a demonstration of God's view of the law and sin and an ultimate victory over all cosmic forces, Christ's paying sinners' penalty is at the heart of the gospel. God's wrath must be assuaged by Jesus as He died on the cross, receiving the punishment that sinners deserved. Christ's sacrifice paid the full penalty for sin, bringing an imputation of God's righteousness and, therefore, full forgiveness. Notice the substitutionary nature of the atonement in these verses, and rejoice in a God who saves:

---

[8]Machen, *Christianity and Liberalism*, 23–24.

For our sake he made him to be sin who knew no sin, so that in him we might become the righteousness of God. (2 Corinthians 5:21)

For all who rely on works of the law are under a curse; for it is written, "Cursed be everyone who does not abide by all things written in the Book of the Law, and do them" . . . Christ redeemed us from the curse of the law by becoming a curse for us—for it is written, "Cursed is everyone who is hanged on a tree." (Galatians 3:10, 13)

He himself bore our sins in his body on the tree, that we might die to sin and live to righteousness. By his wounds you have been healed. (1 Peter 2:24)

For Christ also suffered once for sins, the righteous for the unrighteous, that he might bring us to God, being put to death in the flesh but made alive in the spirit. (1 Peter 3:18)

Surely he has borne our griefs and carried our sorrows; yet we esteemed him stricken, smitten by God, and afflicted. But he was pierced for our transgressions; he was crushed for our iniquities; upon him was the chastisement that brought us peace, and with his wounds we are healed. All we like sheep have gone astray; we have turned—every one—to his own way; and the LORD has laid on him the iniquity of us all. (Isaiah 53:4–6)

In light of penal (penalty) substitution, songwriter Phillip P. Bliss was right when he penned, "In my place condemned he stood, and sealed my pardon with his blood–hallelujah, what a Savior!"[9]

Fifth, the gospel is scriptural. Paul repeats the phrase, "in accordance with the Scriptures," twice in 1 Corinthians 15:3–4. The Messiah's work of salvation was an Old Testament promise. When Paul wants his New Testament reader to think of an exact Old Testament reference, he uses the singular, "Scripture." Since the plural "Scriptures" is used in 1 Corinthians 15, Paul is alluding to what the Old Testament generally taught, namely, that the entire Old Testament bears witness

---

[9]Phillip P. Bliss, "Hallelujah? What a Savior," accessed from http://cyberhymnal. org/htm/h/a/halwasav.htm.

to the saving work of the Messiah, the sin bearer. The atoning work of Jesus was the pinnacle of salvation history that had been disclosed in the Old Testament through direct prophetic references as well as types and shadows like sacrifices. Paul preached to Agrippa,

> To this day I have had the help that comes from God, and so I stand here testifying both to small and great, saying nothing but what the prophets and Moses said would come to pass: that the Christ must suffer and that, by being the first to rise from the dead, he would proclaim light both to our people and to the Gentiles. (Acts 26:22–23)

The warp and woof of the Jewish Bible is saturated with references to the Messiah and His sacrificial work for sinners. Peter, like Paul, proclaimed God's eternal plan would naturally reveal itself in both the Old and New Testaments:

> This Jesus, delivered up according to the definite plan and foreknowledge of God, you crucified and killed by the hands of lawless men. (Acts 2:23)

Sixth, the gospel was confirmed by the resurrection:

> That he was buried, that he was raised on the third day in accordance with the Scriptures. (1 Corinthians 15:4)

The entire fifteenth chapter of 1 Corinthians is devoted to the resurrection of bodies, both Jesus' body and every believer's physical body. Paul states the burial here to confirm the authenticity and conclusiveness of Jesus' death, thereby presenting the resurrection as a true resurrection from the dead. The Father vindicated the work of the Son on Calvary, by raising Jesus from the dead. The resurrection served as a veritable "Amen" to Christ's "It is finished." Was Christ's death satisfactory for sinners? Did the Son please the Father with His mediatorial sacrifice? Was Jesus the sinless Savior dying for sins that were not His own? Yes, yes, yes (cf., Romans 4:25).

1 Corinthians 15:4 utilizes grammar to rivet an important truth to the mind of every Christian, namely the perfect tense which describes the resurrection as a past event but having a lasting and germane consequence on the present and for the future. Christ has been raised from the dead and He is still the One whom God the Father raised from the dead. Jesus is the risen Lord, even now! The substitutionary death and burial

of Jesus occurred at points of time, but Jesus' resurrection continues as a fact. A cursory reading of Acts reveals the importance of preaching the literal, bodily resurrection of Jesus (Acts 9:20–28; 13:30–37; 17:31).

Paul continues to establish the validity of Christ's resurrection by chronicling Christ's initiative in appearing to many Christians:

> And that He appeared to Cephas, then to the twelve. After that He appeared to more than five hundred brethren at one time, most of whom remain until now, but some have fallen asleep; then He appeared to James, then to all the apostles. (1 Corinthians 15:5–7)

This vast army of witnesses fully attests to Christ's resurrection. There is a continuous chain of eyewitnesses who verified the truth of what Paul states. Paul says that even though Christ's resurrection was twenty to twenty-five years ago, some of the witnesses are still alive today, and you can even go and ask them in person.

Is this the gospel that you believe? Is this the gospel that you proclaim? Did you notice that Paul never focused upon "friendship" evangelism when he discussed the gospel? What does that tell you?

Response

1. If you are not a Christian, then repent and believe in the God of such good news!

2. If you are a Christian by the sovereign grace of God, do not ever think that you should move beyond the gospel. Some Christians believe that the gospel was for their salvation, but now they need to move on toward "deeper" topics. Jerry Bridges provides a wake up call for such thinking: "The gospel is not only the most important message in all of history; it is the only essential message in all of history."

3. When you need motivation, ponder the gospel. Spurgeon wrote, "When I thought God was hard, I found it easy to sin: but when I found God so kind, so good, so overflowing with compassion, I smote upon my breast to think that I could ever have rebelled against One who loved me so, and sought my good."

4. Guard the gospel!

John Calvin wisely commented:

> Without the gospel, everything is useless and vain; without the gospel we are not Christians; without the gospel all riches is poverty, all wisdom, folly before God; strength is weakness, and all the justice of man is under the condemnation of God. But by the knowledge of the gospel we are made children of God, brothers of Jesus Christ, fellow townsmen with the saints, citizens of the Kingdom of Heaven, heirs of God with Jesus Christ, by whom the poor are made rich, the weak strong, the fools wise, the sinners justified, the desolate comforted, the doubting sure, and slaves free. The gospel is the word of life and truth. It is the power of God for the salvation of all those who believe, and the key to the knowledge of God, which opens the door of the Kingdom of Heaven to the faithful by releasing them from sins, and closes it to the unbelievers, binding them in their sins. Blessed are all they who hear the gospel and keep it; for in this way they show that they are children of God. Woe to those who will not hear it and follow it; because they are children of the devil.[10]

5. Preach the gospel to your friends.

6. Preach the gospel to your enemies.

7. Remember that you do not need a relationship with someone so that you can preach the gospel.

8. You cannot live the gospel. It must be proclaimed. Jesus is the only one who could live a perfect life. You are not Jesus, so tell people about Jesus, both His active and passive obedience.

---

[10]John Calvin, Preface to Pierre-Robert Olivétan's 1535 translation of the Bible, accessed from http://www.ccel.org/ccel/calvin/calcom.iv.html.

Chapter Two

. . .

White Lie #2: You Just Need More Time

. . .

Many families live their lives like they all work for FedEx delivery service, driving pell-mell, running hither and thither, expecting everything to be "absolutely, positively delivered overnight." Well, minus the nifty uniforms, most followers of Christ (a man who never owned a watch) ape everyone else in the world regarding time and one's relationship to it, hyperventilating all the way to the weekend. Those interested in mastering time, instead of time being the reader's taskmaster, reading the following chapter is an urgent priority! There is no time to lose…

Why are Christians such a frenetic bunch? Yet the words, "hectic" and "chaotic" do not need to typify believers' lives. Surely, no one desires to hear words like these blare from a boisterous megaphone: "Hurry up" and "Don't waste so much time." Would a person's life actually be better if they had more time? Or would they revert to treating 268 hours in a week into what people do with the 168 hours given to them? If people had more quality time with their children and spouse, would the glitches in their lives (and yours) be alleviated? Isn't it about *high time* that Christians had some *time* thinking biblically about *time*?

I present some shocking news that should revolutionize your life: time is actually your ally. Time is your friend. "Time is on your side" (think 1960s song). Time is a gift, granted to you by the Lord of time. God created time and He fixed our days to be exactly twenty-four hours and our weeks to be 168 hours. God's wisdom determined that 167 hours were not the optimum duration for a week, nor did He decree a 38-hour day. Being all-powerful, He could make the sun do whatever He wanted, but 24 hours was His choice because God is also all-wise.

Redeeming the Time, Because the Days Are Evil (Ephesians 5:16, KJV)

Modern advice, even from Christians in the area of time, is erroneous. Regularly, Christians take a verse about a subject, but ignore proper interpretation principles. Ephesians 5:16 is especially misused by many in the church, so pay close attention to the following section. How can time be redeemed? Can time be bought or purchased? If soda bottles were once redeemed by taking them to the recycling machine at the supermarket, how is time redeemed? Some incorrect applications of Ephesians 5:16 are:

- Account for time like a commodity.
- Complain about how short a day is.
- Desire more time.
- Budget time.
- Put clocks in every room.
- Think time is your most valuable asset.
- Stress "quality time" over and against "quantity time."
- Calculate how many of each day's 86,400 seconds you waste.
- Don't waste a minute of the day.
- Time waits for no one.
- Time is money.
- All sins can be forgiven except wastage of time.
- Do not let other people spend your time for you.

Before we look at the meaning of Ephesians 5:16, it is imperative to think of time as the folks in the Bible would have perceived it. How would the readers of the letter to the Ephesian church consider time? Most people reading this book (the one you are holding) will have a Western mindset, so thinking like a person from the East is critical since the Bible is written from an Eastern perspective. People from the East differ from Westerners in many areas, but never so much as they do when relating to time.

The Bible is littered (in a good way) with verses discussing the administration of money and resources, but there is not a whole lot of discussion about time. Why? It is directly related to the culture of the day and their attitude toward time. Easterners did not consider time to be a product to be utilized or to be wasted. Their culture of time focused more on people and relationships than punctuality and precision. People were important, not time.

Robert Banks quipped, "Whereas the English clock runs, the Spanish clock walks."[1] If time is running, we had better go grab it by the tail and tame it. Slow it down. But if time is on a leisurely stroll, we are rightly tempted to go along with it for a stroll. See how different we are today? Does your personal clock sprint or does it saunter? The original audience of every Bible book would be much closer to the Spanish clock mindset.

The Purpose of Time

Is time linear or cyclical? The question is like asking "Is light a particle or a wave?" because the nature of the question tries to limit the answer to parameters that cannot adequately explain the question. Time is cyclical in the sense that there are seasons to everything (Ecclesiastes 3:1–8), but it is also linear with regard to having an ending, a consummation. Jesus said that He was the "Alpha and the Omega, the first and the last, the beginning and the end" (Revelation 22:13). There is an end to time and a consummation to history. There was a beginning in Genesis and there will be an end described in Revelation. *The New Bible Dictionary* is insightful in its description of the concept of time in the Scriptures:

> The Bible thus stresses not the abstract continuity of time but rather the God-given content of certain moments of history. This view of time may be called "linear," in contrast with the cyclical view of time common in the ancient world; God's purpose moves to a consummation; things do not just go on or return to the point whence they began. But calling the biblical view of time "linear" must not be allowed to suggest that time and history flow on in an inevitable succession of events; rather the Bible stresses "times," the points at which God himself advances his purposes in the world.[2]

---

[1] Robert Banks, *The Tyranny of Time: When 24 Hours Is Not Enough* (Downers Grove, IL: InterVarsity Press, 1983), 144.

[2] M. H. Cressey, "Time," *The New Bible Dictionary*, edited by J. D. Douglas (Downers Grove, IL: InterVarsity Press, 1996), 1187.

Simply, the Bible teaches that there is a purpose to time. Time has a purpose. God was unfolding His purpose for the universe and everyone in it. The original readers of the Bible were not reading "redeeming the time" by trying to pack every minute to the brim with godly activity. The most beneficial way to correct the wrong assumptions about being good stewards of time is to look at a different translation of Ephesians 5:16 and to look at the phrase in context. Here is the English Standard Version's translation:

> Look carefully then how you walk, not as unwise but as wise, making the best use of the time, because the days are evil. (Ephesians 5:15–16)

Paul wanted the church at Ephesus to take advantage of opportunities when they came to them. Grab every possible occasion that arises, especially to engage in loving the church and evangelizing the lost. Look at the verse again and notice, "*the* time." Paul does not say, "redeem time." Christians have one life to live; therefore, they must be on the alert to circumstances when they are put in their path by God, the Sovereign King. Paul chooses a word for time that means "the right moment" (*kairos*) and not "duration of time" (*chronos*). Paul was not thinking minutes, hours and days—he was stressing opportunity knocking on your door! Living like the world's clock is about to strike twelve is not what Paul was highlighting. Instead, time is the realm where God's purposes are advanced and furthered. "Thy kingdom come, Thy will be done" kind of time.

Every reader has plenty of time and opportunities for serving during "the time." Each Christian has all the time that God, the Creator of time, wants them to have. During the day, keep a keen eye out for special occasions and opportunities to serve Christ Jesus. Warren Wiersbe wrote, "Our English word *opportunity* comes from the Latin and means 'towards the port.' It suggest a ship taking advantage of the wind and tide to arrive safely in the harbor."[3] If believers are sitting around fretting about all the minutes they are wasting, they just might be blinded to the ministry opportunity that the Lord is dropping into their proverbial laps. Redeem "the time," not "time."

Divine Interruptions

Let's apply this to interruptions. Even the concept of interruption goes against Ephesians 5:16. From the human perspective, interruptions

---

[3]Warren Wiersbe, *Be Rich* (Colorado Springs: David C. Cook, 1979), 142.

"interrupt" us and take time away from something else. But from God's vantage point, all interruptions are divinely ordained. More than that, most interruptions are opportunities for Christians to obey Ephesians 5:16 and "redeem the time."

Reflect on the life of the Lord Jesus. How did Christ react to "interruptions"? Read the following portion of Mark 5 carefully and with "time" and "the time" in mind:

> And when Jesus had crossed again in the boat to the other side, a great crowd gathered about him, and he was beside the sea. Then came one of the rulers of the synagogue, Jairus by name, and seeing him, he fell at his feet and implored him earnestly, saying, "My little daughter is at the point of death. Come and lay your hands on her, so that she may be made well and live." And he went with him.

> And a great crowd followed him and thronged about him. And there was a woman who had had a discharge of blood for twelve years, and who had suffered much under many physicians, and had spent all that she had, and was no better but rather grew worse. She had heard the reports about Jesus and came up behind him in the crowd and touched his garment. For she said, "If I touch even his garments, I will be made well." And immediately the flow of blood dried up, and she felt in her body that she was healed of her disease. And Jesus, perceiving in himself that power had gone out from him, immediately turned about in the crowd and said, "Who touched my garments?" And his disciples said to him, "You see the crowd pressing around you, and yet you say, 'Who touched me?'" And he looked around to see who had done it. But the woman, knowing what had happened to her, came in fear and trembling and fell down before him and told him the whole truth. And he said to her, "Daughter, your faith has made you well; go in peace, and be healed of your disease."

> While he was still speaking, there came from the ruler's house some who said, "Your daughter is dead. Why trouble the Teacher any further?" But overhearing what they said, Jesus said to the ruler of the synagogue, "Do not fear, only believe." And he allowed no one to follow him except

Peter and James and John the brother of James. They came to the house of the ruler of the synagogue, and Jesus saw a commotion, people weeping and wailing loudly. And when he had entered, he said to them, "Why are you making a commotion and weeping? The child is not dead but sleeping." And they laughed at him. But he put them all outside and took the child's father and mother and those who were with him and went in where the child was. Taking her by the hand he said to her, "Talitha cumi," which means, "Little girl, I say to you, arise." And immediately the girl got up and began walking (for she was twelve years of age), and they were immediately overcome with amazement. And he strictly charged them that no one should know this, and told them to give her something to eat. (Mark 5:21–43)

Jesus was on His way to a very important ministry opportunity—Jairus' daughter had a pressing and urgent physical need. There is more to be learned from Mark 5, but it does display for us the way Jesus dealt with time and interruptions. God the Father placed the woman with the issue of blood directly in the path of Jesus. Jesus, to use the concept and language of Ephesians 5:16, "redeemed the time." In other words, there was an opportunity to minister and Jesus seized it!

It is a wonder of wonders that the Eternal Son of God inserted Himself into time. Jesus, the God who has always existed, had twenty-four hours a day to minister. Jesus' life reflected purpose, but He was never rushed. He knew the Father was sovereign and Christ lived His life under that umbrella. Redeeming the time, or being a good steward of the time, means that we must focus on actively living in the presence of God, knowing the Lord is purposely acting and guiding our lives and circumstances. Commentator Luck echoes this sentiment: "One of the greatest sins of our modern day is that of simply leaving God out of our lives. We talk and plan and act as if our lives were entirely our own affair, and there were no great God in the heavens. This is practical atheism."[4]

I am not saying that people should waste time. I am not advocating laziness. I think Christians should plan their days, weeks, and years. Procrastination is a waste. My point is to have Ephesians 5:16 capture the reader's mind so that every saint will live in light of making the most of every opportunity.

---

[4]G. Coleman Luck, *James, Faith in Action* (Chicago: Moody Publishing, 1967), 96.

See time as an ally, something that the Lord uses to yield occasions to serve Him and others.

Everyone gets the exact amount of chronological time (525,600 minutes in each year), but not everyone receives the same amount of opportunities from the Lord in the day, so quit looking at your watch and be faithful to the ministry before your eyes. If you are late for a meeting because of an opportunity to serve someone, simply call ahead and inform the person. Stewards must be faithful. If you think of time in minutes only, it is extremely taxing to be faithful to an inert measurement of a day. Weird! But the desire to be faithful to a God-ordained ministry opportunity reverberates the true meaning of Ephesians 5:16 and faithfulness to Jesus Christ.

Being a good steward of time accepts the fact that God is the Creator of everything and He therefore owns what He has made. You are not your own. God made you. Furthermore, Jesus Christ has bought you with His death on Calvary's cross. He ransomed you. Jesus did not die for time. Nothing in the Bible makes sense until Genesis 1:1 has been believed, "In the beginning, God created the heavens and the earth." God ordained both chronological time and the ministry opportunities He presents in our lives. He ordained the length of the day and ordained how many days you will be alive. God owns time. God purposely controls "the time" too.

Lest you think that the Bible only teaches "opportunity time" and never "chronological time," read Psalm 90 and think of biblical time in the way you used to (but just don't think of Ephesians 5:16):

> Lord, you have been our dwelling place
>
> > in all generations.
>
> Before the mountains were brought forth,
>
> > or ever you had formed the earth and the world,
> >
> > from everlasting to everlasting you are God.
>
> You return man to dust
>
> > and say, "Return, O children of man!"
>
> For a thousand years in your sight
>
> > are but as yesterday when it is past,
> >
> > or as a watch in the night.

You sweep them away as with a flood; they are like a dream,

> like grass that is renewed in the morning:

> in the morning it flourishes and is renewed;

> in the evening it fades and withers.

For we are brought to an end by your anger;

> by your wrath we are dismayed.

You have set our iniquities before you,

> our secret sins in the light of your presence.

For all our days pass away under your wrath;

> we bring our years to an end like a sigh.

The years of our life are seventy,

> or even by reason of strength eighty;

> yet their span is but toil and trouble;

> they are soon gone, and we fly away.

Who considers the power of your anger,

> and your wrath according to the fear of you?

So teach us to number our days

> that we may get a heart of wisdom.

Return, O LORD! How long?

> Have pity on your servants!

Satisfy us in the morning with your steadfast love,

> that we may rejoice and be glad all our days.

Make us glad for as many days as you have afflicted us,

> and for as many years as we have seen evil.

Let your work be shown to your servants,

> and your glorious power to their children.

Let the favor of the Lord our God be upon us,

> and establish the work of our hands upon us;

> yes, establish the work of our hands!

Psalm 90

In this sense, Jonathan Edwards' resolution makes sense: "Resolved: never to lose one moment of time, but to improve it in the most profitable way I possibly can." Psalm 90 teaches us that the Eternal God loves frail and sinful humans; therefore, you should have the desire to make your life count for God. Every day is a birthday since we are taught to "number our days" in verse 12. Birthdays every day—yes, but when an opportunity to serve someone comes up on your birthday, quickly blow out the candles and "redeem the time!"

Conclusion

For Christians, time has morphed from Mr. Hyde in the Bible to Dr. Jekyll in our fast-paced, high-tech century. Time is something neutral and fixed, yet it has become a slave driver and stern taskmaster. Actually, time is a gracious gift to us from our Triune God. Serve the Lord and not time. Be content with the 24-hour day.

For those who have failed to be good stewards of time, rejoice that there is a Substitute. In the Garden, Jesus prayed, "I glorified you on earth, having accomplished the work that you gave me to do. And now, Father, glorify me in your own presence with the glory that I had with you before the world existed" (John 17:4–5). Christians have Christ's perfect obedience credited to their spiritual bank account so that God the Father sees all Christians as always redeeming the time. What a Savior we have. It's about time to think rightly about time.

Response

1. Pray that the Lord would let you react to interruptions like Christ did.

2. Pray for the recognition of God-ordained ministry opportunities.

3. Read the Scriptures so that you get an "Eastern" (not Eastern mysticism, but the Near Eastern way of life) feel for time (Grant Horner's Bible reading program is the best).[5]

4. In ministry at your local church, do **not** manage by objectives. Your goal should be to honor Jesus by shepherding people **as** you try to reach the goal in ministry.

---

[5]http://www.biblestudytools.com/bible-reading-plan/prof-horners-reading-system.html.

Quotes on Time

"Time is God's way of keeping everything from happening at once."

"Men talk of killing time, while time quietly kills them."

"Calendars are for careful people, not passionate ones."

"Oh! Do not attack me with your watch. A watch is always too fast or too slow. I cannot be dictated to by a watch."

"We must use time as a tool, not as a crutch."[6]

[6]Accessed from http://www.quotationspage.com/subjects/time/.

Chapter Three

' ' '

White Lie #3: Christians Must Tithe

' ' '

Will man rob God? Yet you are robbing me. But you say, "How have we robbed you?" In your tithes and contributions. (Malachi 3:8)

"Stick 'em up!" Words that no one on an isolated, dark street corner ever wishes to hear. Who could ever fathom that a Bible verse would be used for a similar, spiritual burglary? But that is exactly what occurs in more churches than you might imagine. Malachi 3:8 has a long barrel and packs quite a punch to the non-suspecting congregant. But sadly, God is not the one who is robbed of what is His. Instead, the naïve person sitting in the pew is bamboozled out of God's truth. The biblical management of money never needs to resort to wrenching Bible verses out of context to get people to give money to the Lord's work.

The first concept that needs to be understood as we consider tithing (offering a tenth) is that there is a difference between Old Testament/Covenant giving and New Testament/Covenant giving. The Old Testament required Israelites to give the Lord's Tithe (Leviticus 27:30), Festival Tithes (Deuteronomy 12:10–11, 17–18) and, on top of all that, Poor Tithes (Deuteronomy 14:28–29), a variety of taxes (Nehemiah 10:32–39), and other offerings (Numbers 18:11–13; Exodus 25:1–2). Would Christians rather give 10 percent, even of their gross income, or would they like to give what those in the nation of Israel had to give, which, added together, was well over 25%? Beware of people wielding Old Testament verses out of context. Beware of teachers who do not know the difference between Israel and the church.

Even in the New Testament, believers must put on their thinking caps when interpreting Bible passages. For example, Christians need to know that when tithing is mentioned in the New Testament, it always refers to the nation of Israel and not the church (Matthew 23:23; Luke 11:42, 18:12; Hebrews 7:5–6, 8–9).

What is the New Testament's percentage for giving? The answer is pretty shocking. It might even jolt Bible readers back into the Old Testament era! The percentage for New Testament giving is 100%. Yes—100%. Feel better? At least it is a round and even number and easy enough to remember. But I am certain that every reader requests biblical proof. In the context of giving, Paul wrote,

> We want you to know, brothers, about the grace of God that has been given among the churches of Macedonia, for in a severe test of affliction, their abundance of joy and their extreme poverty have overflowed in a wealth of generosity on their part. For they gave according to their means, as I can testify, and beyond their means, of their own accord, begging us earnestly for the favor of taking part in the relief of the saints—and this, not as we expected, but they gave themselves first to the Lord and then by the will of God to us. (2 Corinthians 8:1–5)

Notice the number? Or lack of number? The churches of Macedonia begged Paul to let them give generously. It is usually the preacher imploring the listeners to give more abundantly. The crux of the matter was that these saints "gave themselves first to the Lord." The number is 100%. Is this your attitude? Have you given yourself first to the Lord? The puzzle of sacrificial giving is solved by totally dedicating oneself to the Lord Jesus. *If Jesus possesses you, then He owns all you own, including all your money.* Show me a person not sold out to their Creator and I will show you a person who struggles with sacrificial giving. Show me a Christian who is wholly devoted to the Lord Jesus and I will show you a person who thinks rightly about money.

It's All His

Actually, the Lord does not need money—not yours or anyone else's. Furthermore, God does not primarily want your money. God wants you. Romans 12:1 presents the same concept: "I appeal to you therefore, brothers, by the mercies of God, to present your bodies as a living sacrifice, holy and acceptable to God, which is your spiritual worship." In light of the wonderful grace and mercy of the Triune God explained in Romans 1–11, Paul understands that the only logical response to such a great salvation is to yield your entire being to the work of Christ Jesus. The focus on money and percentages is too myopic and too small. God wants you. All of you.

Instead of searching for and defaulting to a New Testament giving percentage, there is more to consider than a number. God wants followers of Christ to use their minds and to have rational and spiritual reasons for doing what they do. When Christians give their money to a local church, they are ultimately giving to God Himself. For example, the question of "what is the least I can give?" needs to be thoughtfully replaced with "to whom am I giving?" Philippians 4:18 demonstrates that Paul taught that giving is not to the pastor, building, missionary, or anyone else—it is to God:

> I have received full payment, and more. I am well supplied, having received from Epaphroditus the gifts you sent, a fragrant offering, a sacrifice acceptable and pleasing to God.

David Livingston thoughtfully reflected upon the fact that all giving is ultimately contributing to the Lord and His work. The African missionary preached, "I place no value on anything I have or may possess, except in relation to the kingdom of God. If anything will advance the interests of the kingdom, it shall be given away or kept, only as by giving or keeping it I shall most promote the glory of Him to whom I owe all my hopes in time or eternity."[1]

It is all God's money anyway, so it makes perfect sense that we give "our" money to the Lord. God owns everything, yet He desires His children to be faithful stewards of what He owns and what He has given them to manage. Haggai 2:8 is emphatic:

> The silver is mine, and the gold is mine, declares the LORD of hosts.

Therefore, how are you handling God's money? What account will

---

[1]William Garden Blakie, *The Personal Life of David Livingstone: Chiefly from His Unpublished Journals and Correspondence in the Possession of His Family* (London: Harper Brothers, 1881), 139.

you, the steward, give to the Lord on the Great Day when accounting tallies will yield the numbers and the motivation for your financial decisions?

It is helpful to grasp the truth that every talent, natural ability, and gift people possess are from the generous hand of God. People are able to work because of the Lord's working in their life. Their mind, body, skills, and experience are not because they are self-made men or women. Rather, their résumé is a summary of how wonderfully and uniquely God has orchestrated their life. What was true for Israel is true for each follower of Jesus Christ; namely, that the ability they have to make money is a gift from the Lord. Moses said,

> You shall remember the LORD your God, for it is he who gives you power to get wealth, that he may confirm his covenant that he swore to your fathers, as it is this day. (Deuteronomy 8:18)

. Furthermore, it is imperative to consider that money is temporal—it does not last. Think of a loaf of bread, especially the healthy whole-grain kind. If you do not use it in a couple of days, it goes bad. It has a limited shelf life. In a similar fashion, money has a shelf life. It cannot be taken to heaven, and even if it could, it would not be needed because there is no need for money in heaven. Spend it on the earth or it cannot be spent at all. Solomon wrote, "for riches do not last forever; and does a crown endure to all generations?" (Proverbs 27:24). Moldy money, like moldy bread, is not good for anything except for bird food. Jesus elaborated on the same truth saying:

> Do not lay up for yourselves treasures on earth, where moth and rust destroy and where thieves break in and steal, but lay up for yourselves treasures in heaven, where neither moth nor rust destroys and where thieves do not break in and steal. For where your treasure is, there your heart will be also. (Matthew 6:19–21)

Paul provides his readers an added incentive for liberal and generous giving:

> The point is this: whoever sows sparingly will also reap sparingly, and whoever sows bountifully will also reap bountifully. Each one must give as he has decided in his heart, not reluctantly or under compulsion, for God loves a cheerful giver. (2 Corinthians 9:6–7)

Paul sheds light on the question, "How much shall I give?" without ever talking percentages or exact amounts. Why are people so stressed about the number and percentage? All too often, numbers bypass the heart and how people should deal with the true motivation for what they do or don't do. The principle in 2 Corinthians 9 is simple: if you slip God a wooden nickel (something minimal or essentially worthless), guess what you get back? You receive in kind. Therefore, God commands cheerful giving so that you can be the recipient of His cheerful giving back to you. Because of that, God needs no gimmicks, pledges, or talk of matching funds. God calls for simple and voluntary giving. When leaders pressure congregants and verbally, or otherwise, coerce their flock to give with sadness or grief (this would be classified as "reluctantly"), you should immediately know that their methods are not biblical. Actually, the leaders are robbing God of the true meaning of giving in the Sacred Scriptures.

Love Gives

God loves. God loves people. God loves sinful people. In what manner does God display His love for us? By giving! Observe the outpouring of our loving God:

> For God so loved the world, that he gave his only Son, that whoever believes in him should not perish but have eternal life. (John 3:16)

> But God shows his love for us in that while we were still sinners, Christ died for us. (Romans 5:8)

God's greatest demonstration of love was the fact that He gave His sinless Son to die a sinner's death on our behalf. God did not have to give His Son to us. We merited only His wrath, but we freely received, out of His eternal love, Christ's life as our Representative and His death as our Substitute. It was such a great gift that God punctuated the atoning work of Jesus by raising Him from the dead! Christians have been ransomed at a great cost. People who have received generous outpourings of love should not grasp money with a white knuckled grip. Since God was not parsimonious with His Son, how can we respond to Him with giving that could only be described as stingy? Who can think of numbers and percentages when we consider Christ's redemption on Calvary? He fully (100%) gave Himself. He did not give 50%. He did not give 90%. To quote a popular hymn, "Jesus paid it all, all to Him I owe, sin had left a crimson stain, He washed it white as snow."

How Much Is Enough?

The next time a Christian or a pastor pulls out Malachi 3:8 and points it at your wallet, be thankful that you know the real truth, dismissing the weapon like you would a realistic looking water or cap gun. "Bang!" Christians should never give because they are the recipients of Old Testament verses used as leverage.

Jesus, to continue with the analogy of guns, was not robbed. Jesus was the willing recipient of a firing squad. We should have been blindfolded. We should have had our hands tied. Our persons should have been tightly tied to the pole. We should have been trembling as we heard the fateful words, "Ready, aim, fire!" Thankfully, our Savior stood in front of the holy bullets of the wrath of Almighty God. By making propitiation, Jesus absorbed all the punishment we had earned when we broke God's holy laws. In light of that truth, I hope you give differently this Sunday.

> For you know the grace of our Lord Jesus Christ, that though he was rich, yet for your sake he became poor, so that you by his poverty might become rich. (2 Corinthians 8:9)

Response

1. Think. Consider. Reflect. Do not default to the temptation to pick a number for your giving just to "get that out of the way." Regularly cogitate on what you have deserved as a sinner and then rejoice at what God earned for you through the person and work of Jesus Christ, the God-Man.

2. Do not let anyone bully you with verses from Scripture intended for the nation of Israel. Warning, red alert!

3. Ten percent is certainly a good place to start when it comes to New Testament giving, but don't call it a "tithe" and do not think you are under Mosaic Law. Your mind matters.

4. Pray that the Lord would grant to you the philosophy of Oswald Chambers who uttered, "It's not what you give, but what you do not give that is the true test."

5. Read the Parable of the Talents and ask the Lord to perform some heart surgery on you, so that you might be a faithful steward of all that the Lord has given you, especially money.

> For it will be like a man going on a journey, who called his servants and entrusted to them his property. To one he

gave five talents, to another two, to another one, to each according to his ability. Then he went away. He who had received the five talents went at once and traded with them, and he made five talents more. So also he who had the two talents made two talents more. But he who had received the one talent went and dug in the ground and hid his master's money. Now after a long time the master of those servants came and settled accounts with them. And he who had received the five talents came forward, bringing five talents more, saying, "Master, you delivered to me five talents; here I have made five talents more." His master said to him, "Well done, good and faithful servant. You have been faithful over a little; I will set you over much. Enter into the joy of your master." And he also who had the two talents came forward, saying, "Master, you delivered to me two talents; here I have made two talents more." His master said to him, "Well done, good and faithful servant. You have been faithful over a little; I will set you over much. Enter into the joy of your master." He also who had received the one talent came forward, saying, "Master, I knew you to be a hard man, reaping where you did not sow, and gathering where you scattered no seed, so I was afraid, and I went and hid your talent in the ground. Here you have what is yours." But his master answered him, "You wicked and slothful servant! You knew that I reap where I have not sown and gather where I scattered no seed? Then you ought to have invested my money with the bankers, and at my coming I should have received what was my own with interest. So take the talent from him and give it to him who has the ten talents. For to everyone who has will more be given, and he will have an abundance. But from the one who has not, even what he has will be taken away. And cast the worthless servant into the outer darkness. In that place there will be weeping and gnashing of teeth." (Matthew 25:14–30)

6. Give liberally so that others glorify God! If you have ever received a wonderful gift, then your proper response should be, "Thank you." When Christians cheerfully give, they both glorify God and serve as a catalyst for others to do the same.

For the ministry of this service is not only supplying the needs of the saints but is also overflowing in many thanksgivings to God. By their approval of this service, they will glorify God because of your submission that comes from your confession of the gospel of Christ, and the generosity of your contribution for them and for all others, while they long for you and pray for you, because of the surpassing grace of God upon you. Thanks be to God for his inexpressible gift! (2 Corinthians 9:12–15)

7. Make sure the main recipient of your giving is your local church. If you want to give to other ministries, make them secondary. In other words, give to para-church ministries only with an "above and beyond" attitude.

Chapter Four

' ' '

White Lie #4: Missionaries Must Suffer to Stay Humble

' ' '

Plastered onto my long-term memory is a haunting morning spent in Asia. Since that day, my mind has regularly done a series of gut-check contortions. I was visiting a missionary family that our church supported and I wanted to get to know them and their ministry better. At least I initially thought I did. After twenty hours of flight time, I arrived at their home and fell asleep for a few hours. I yawningly woke to the smell of breakfast being prepared. It smelled amazingly wonderful. The aroma seeped into my bedroom and literally reenergized me. Say goodbye to jetlag! I entered the kitchen and was greeted by the person responsible for the graciously prepared food. But the person was not "our" missionary. It was not his wife and it was not one of his children. The missionary's maid prepared the food. Yes, the maid. The breakfast seemed stuck in my throat. "Do you have any antacid?"

Maybe I could see hiring someone to clean the house once a week, but a maid who also functioned as their cook? Hey, wait a minute, I don't even have a maid, or a cook, or a house cleaner, or the array of yummy spices being used to complete the preparation of the meal. I tabled my conscience for a few pleasantries and then wolfed down the savory dish. The zesty food was scrumptious, but my mind had missionary heartburn (would that technically be mind burn?). Back in my room the questions returned, but this time, with a tsunami-like force. Actually, THE question bellowed in my mind, "Are we sending money for overseas missions so that people can have maids and cooks?"

I experienced what many other people think about missions. I call it the "myth of missions." The legend and folklore of said myth goes something like this: the church cuts a check once a month and sends it to a mission agency, which then distributes the money to the missionaries. In return, once every three to six months, the missionary sends a cool, electronic "update letter." Lest I forget some of the lore, the local church sees the missionary for two days when they are on their furlough. Missions 101 in a nutshell! The church gets to feel good for supporting gospel work, and the missionaries get support. A match made in…

A Double Standard

Why were thoughts of envy flooding my mind and not deliberations of joy for my missionary friends? Because I thought exactly how many, or dare I say most, Christians think about missions today. My view of being a good steward of the missionaries our church supported was torqued. It was selfish. It was not biblical. And of all people I should have known better. As a pastor, I should have been able to identify with the oversea servants because the same local church pays my salary and I spend the money on more than Bible commentaries and gospel tracts. If the truth were told, I use some of the money on ice cream for my family and regularly treat myself to $4 coffee. I go on vacations, purchase carbon bike equipment, and I would even hire a cook and maid if the price were right. (If you must know, the reason our missionary family can hire a maid is because maids are very inexpensive in that country, so that it is no big financial issue at all).

Put another way, do you like new clothes? Fashionable clothes? Do your children enjoy swimming lessons? Are you "for" or "against" vacations and holidays? Is "splurge" or "treat" in your vocabulary? Of course! And there is no reason for you to feel bad about it, unless you are sinfully hedonistic. And there must be no reason for you to harbor any type of negative feelings for missionaries doing what you do where you live. They just do it overseas with a different currency.

Rather than feeling guilty *for treating ourselves or being annoyed* when missionaries we support are extravagant, we should change our view of missions.

The older missionaries would ship their children to boarding schools so that they could pour themselves out for gospel work. What heartbreak, and what a tragedy! The modern-day calamity is that most congregants treat their missionaries like *they* are at boarding schools. Even on furlough, missionaries are rarely embraced like family members and as part of the local flock. Soccer practice and the television drown out almost everything, including remembering the missionary children's names.

The great news, which needs to be riveted to the soul of every Christian, is that the concepts for right thinking about the care of missionaries, and then right doing, are not complicated at all. They are within our grasp. Actually, they are in this very chapter! We do not need to know the Coptic language to excel in serving missionaries. The rest of the chapter breaks down into two sections: first, is the simple development of some basic building blocks of missions; second, some practical exhortations and ideas to give us a better understanding of the missionary mindset. For budding theologians, let's begin with doctrine and end with duty. Creed is the engine pulling the caboose of conduct. Credenda (belief) followed by agenda (behavior). This is a very Pauline paradigm, indeed!

Building Blocks of Missions Care

It is essential that we begin with some building blocks of the philosophy of missionary care. General concepts should assist us in the understanding of missions so that our thinking in this area might increase for God's glory. Six exhortations are designed to be purposeful truths calculated to help us think rightly about missions and grace-empowered commitments toward our missionaries.

1. Remember that Jesus was a missionary.

Missionary means "one who is sent on a mission." The Father, in eternity past, agreeing with the Son and the Holy Spirit, decided to send Jesus into the world to live a perfect life and then to die a substitutionary death so that all who believe in Him might have forgiveness of their sins and the hope of being with the Risen King in heaven.

At the risk of overkill, it will help us to read every verse in the Gospel according to John that makes explicit that Jesus was *sent*! As we read these passages, it is important that we ask the Lord to increase our appreciation of Jesus, the sent One. As our appreciation for Jesus the missionary goes up, so will our concept of every other gospel-oriented missionary (emphases added):

> Jesus said to them, "My food is to do the will of him who
> *sent* me and to accomplish his work." (John 4:34)

That all may honor the Son, just as they honor the Father. Whoever does not honor the Son does not honor the Father who *sent* him. (John 5:23)

Truly, truly, I say to you, whoever hears my word and believes him who *sent* me has eternal life. He does not come into judgment, but has passed from death to life. (John 5:24)

I can do nothing on my own. As I hear, I judge, and my judgment is just, because I seek not my own will but the will of him who *sent* me. (John 5:30)

But the testimony that I have is greater than that of John. For the works that the Father has given me to accomplish, the very works that I am doing, bear witness about me that the Father has *sent* me. (John 5:36)

And the Father who *sent* me has himself borne witness about me. His voice you have never heard, his form you have never seen, and you do not have his word abiding in you, for you do not believe the one whom he has *sent*. (John 5:37–38)

Jesus answered them, "This is the work of God, that you believe in him whom he has *sent*." (John 6:29)

For I have come down from heaven, not to do my own will but the will of him who *sent* me. And this is the will of him who *sent* me, that I should lose nothing of all that he has given me, but raise it up on the last day. (John 6:38–39)

No one can come to me unless the Father who *sent* me draws him. And I will raise him up on the last day. (John 6:44)

As the living Father *sent* me, and I live because of the Father, so whoever feeds on me, he also will live because of me. (John 6:57)

So Jesus answered them, "My teaching is not mine, but his who *sent* me." (John 7:16)

The one who speaks on his own authority seeks his own glory; but the one who seeks the glory of him who *sent* him is true, and in him there is no falsehood. (John 7:18)

So Jesus proclaimed, as he taught in the temple, "You know me, and you know where I come from. But I have not come of my own accord. He who *sent* me is true, and him you do not know." (John 7:28)

I know him, for I come from him, and he *sent* me. (John 7:29)

Jesus then said, "I will be with you a little longer, and then I am going to him who *sent* me." (John 7:33)

Yet even if I do judge, my judgment is true, for it is not I alone who judge, but I and the Father who *sent* me. (John 8:16)

I am the one who bears witness about myself, and the Father who *sent* me bears witness about me. (John 8:18)

I have much to say about you and much to judge, but he who *sent* me is true, and I declare to the world what I have heard from him. (John 8:26)

And he who *sent* me is with me. He has not left me alone, for I always do the things that are pleasing to him. (John 8:29)

Jesus said to them, "If God were your Father, you would love me, for I came from God and I am here. I came not of my own accord, but he *sent* me." (John 8:42)

We must work the works of him who *sent* me while it is day; night is coming, when no one can work. (John 9:4)

Do you say of him whom the Father consecrated and *sent* into the world, "You are blaspheming," because I said, "I am the Son of God?" (John 10:36)

I knew that you always hear me, but I said this on account of the people standing around, that they may believe that you *sent* me." (John 11:42)

And Jesus cried out and said, "Whoever believes in me, believes not in me but in him who *sent* me. And whoever sees me sees him who *sent* me." (John 12:44–45)

"For I have not spoken on my own authority, but the Father who *sent* me has himself given me a commandment—what to say and what to speak." (John 12:49)

Truly, truly, I say to you, whoever receives the one I send receives me, and whoever receives me receives the one who *sent* me. (John 13:20)

Whoever does not love me does not keep my words. And the word that you hear is not mine but the Father's who *sent* me. (John 14:24)

But all these things they will do to you on account of my name, because they do not know him who *sent* me. (John 15:21)

But now I am going to him who *sent* me, and none of you asks me, "Where are you going?" (John 16:5)

And this is eternal life, that they know you the only true God, and Jesus Christ whom you have *sent*. (John 17:3)

For I have given them the words that you gave me, and they have received them and have come to know in truth that I came from you; and they have believed that you *sent* me. (John 17:8)

That they may all be one, just as you, Father, are in me, and I in you, that they also may be in us, so that the world may believe that you have *sent* me. (John 17:21)

I in them and you in me, that they may become perfectly one, so that the world may know that you *sent* me and loved them even as you loved me. (John 17:23)

O righteous Father, even though the world does not know you, I know you, and these know that you have *sent* me. (John 17:25)

Jesus was *sent*! The practical Christian life is inextricably linked to keeping the focus on the Lord Jesus Christ, the sent One. Everything is seen properly when Jesus is the center of the Christian's focus and affections. Albert Barnes offers a helpful way to stay motivated for Christian service and to prevent myopia:

> I entreat you to devote one solemn hour of thought to a crucified Savior, a Savior expiring in the bitterest agony. Think of the cross, the nails, the open wounds, the anguish of His soul. Think how the Son of God became a man of sorrows and acquainted with grief that you might live forever. Think as you lie down upon your bed to rest, how your Savior was lifted up from the earth to die. Think amid your plans and anticipations of future gaiety, what the redemption of your soul has cost, and how the dying Savior would wish you to act. His wounds plead that you will live for better things.[1]

It does not take a seminary professor to see the relationship between Jesus the Missionary and the implications for oversight of missionaries. However, for some clarification, the second point makes the implicit, explicit.

2. Acknowledge that King Jesus Himself has sent all Christian missionaries.

Jesus prayed to His Father in the garden, "As you sent me into the world, so I have sent them into the world" (John 17:18). These words were directly intended for the disciples, yet they have far-reaching effects for every missionary today. The same is true of what we know as the Great Commission:

> And Jesus came and said to them, "All authority in heaven and on earth has been given to me. Go therefore and make disciples of all nations, baptizing them in the name of the Father and of the Son and of the Holy Spirit, teaching them to observe all that I have commanded you. And behold, I am with you always, to the end of the age." (Matthew 28:18–20)

Since Jesus Himself has sent out modern day missionaries, how shall we treat them? There is a direct correlation between honoring the One

---

[1]Charles Noel Douglas, *Forty Thousand Quotations* (London: George G. Harrap & Co. LTD., 1904), 279.

sending by honoring those whom He sent. Jesus said,

> When the Son of Man comes in his glory, and all the angels with him, then he will sit on his glorious throne. Before him will be gathered all the nations, and he will separate people one from another as a shepherd separates the sheep from the goats. And he will place the sheep on his right, but the goats on the left. Then the King will say to those on his right, "Come, you who are blessed by my Father, inherit the kingdom prepared for you from the foundation of the world. For I was hungry and you gave me food, I was thirsty and you gave me drink, I was a stranger and you welcomed me, I was naked and you clothed me, I was sick and you visited me, I was in prison and you came to me." Then the righteous will answer him, saying, "Lord, when did we see you hungry and feed you, or thirsty and give you drink? And when did we see you a stranger and welcome you, or naked and clothe you? And when did we see you sick or in prison and visit you?" And the King will answer them, "Truly, I say to you, as you did it to one of the least of these my brothers, you did it to me." (Matthew 25:31–40)

Bible scholar William Hendriksen echoed the words of Jesus stating, "Whatever was done for Christ's disciples, out of love for Christ, is counted as if done for Christ."[2] Epaphroditus was truly doing the work of Christ as he served Paul the missionary. Philippians 2:30 says, "for he [Epaphroditus] nearly died for the work of Christ, risking his life to complete what was lacking in your service to me." Time has not changed the outcome of supporting missionaries. When you serve gospel-centered missionaries today, you are actually doing the work of Christ.

A.T. Pierson wrote,

> Whatever is done for God, without respect of its comparative character as related to other acts, is service, and only that is service. Service is, comprehensively speaking, doing the will of God. He is the object. All is for Him, for His sake, as unto the Lord, not as unto man. Hence, even the humblest act of humblest disciple acquires a certain

---

[2]William Hendricksen, *Exposition of the Gospel According to Matthew* (Grand Rapids, MI: Baker, 1973), 880.

divine quality by its being done with reference to Him. The supreme test of service is this: "For whom am I doing this?" Much that we call service to Christ is not such at all. . . . If we are doing this for Christ, we shall not care for human reward or even recognition. Our work must again be tested by three propositions: Is it work from God, as given us to do from Him; for God, as finding in Him its secret of power; and with God, as only a part of His work in which we engage as co-workers with Him.[3]

3. Think rightly about stewardship.

At the most basic meaning, stewardship involves taking care of someone else's property. In Genesis 39, Joseph managed Potiphar's household. I submit that church members should be more motivated to serve their missionaries because the missionaries are someone else's property. God not only created them (and sent them), but He gave them eternal life and has bought them with a price ("Or do you not know that your body is a temple of the Holy Spirit within you, whom you have from God? You are not your own, for you were bought with a price. So glorify God in your body" 1 Corinthians 6:19–20). How do you take care of God's property?

1 Corinthians 4:2 declares, "Moreover, it is required of stewards that they be found faithful." What a relief it is to be relieved of any pressure to be found innovative, pioneering, rich, or novel. Stewardship is responsible faithfulness of someone else's property.

4. Admire Christians who sacrifice much for the Lord.

I admire men and women who have sacrificed much for the One who sacrificed Himself. Ignore the media created "heroes" and lock onto men and women who serve the only Hero. Admiration breeds affection, which yields love.

> I have held many things in my hand, and have lost them all;
> but whatever I have placed in God's hands, that I still possess.
> —Martin Luther

> I place no value on anything I have or may possess, except
> in relation to the kingdom of God. If anything will advance
> the interests of the kingdom, it shall be given away or kept,

---

[3] Accessed from http://www.sermonillustrations.com/a-z/s/service.htm.

only as by giving or keeping it I shall most promote the glory of Him to whom I owe all my hopes in time or eternity.
—David Livingstone[4]

5. Make a wholesale commitment to serve missionaries.

Make room in your hearts for us . . . . (2 Corinthians 7:2a)

Paul pleaded with the Corinthians to accept him in their hearts. "To make room" in a house would require some cleaning, rearrangement, and a trip to the Goodwill, or in some cases, the dump. In a figurative fashion, Paul specifically wants his readers to push the false teachers away and into the proverbial dump. He wants the readers to make some room for him in their hearts. The idea of "making room" is valuable for the consideration of being good stewards of missionaries because our hearts are cluttered and full of way too much "stuff." We conscientious congregants need to take a load of self, sin, and the world to the dump in order to rid ourselves of our preoccupation with self. Making room for missionaries in one's heart will yield the same kind of feelings one experiences when the house is finally cleaned and the excess junk is successfully delivered to the recycling center, but better. Ah!

6. Don't wait for the church to serve her missionaries—you are the church.

When your church supports missionaries, that means you (and I) support them indirectly through giving. True enough. But, if we are concerned that the church does not do enough for their needs and support, remember that you are the church. Instead of complaining about the leadership or the missions committee, act! Peter charges his readers,

> As each has received a gift, use it to serve one another, as good stewards of God's varied grace: whoever speaks, as one who speaks oracles of God; whoever serves, as one who serves by the strength that God supplies—in order that in everything God may be glorified through Jesus Christ. To him belong glory and dominion forever and ever. Amen. (1 Peter 4:10–11)

Your service and ministry should reflect how much you treasure

[4]Charles Noel Douglas, *Forty Thousand Quotations* (London: George G. Harrap & Co. LTD., 1904), 279.

God's grace. You are one of the "each" who Peter talks about. Keep on employing your gift by serving others, including your missionaries. What is holding you back?

Practical Considerations

What can the church specifically do to help her members embrace a biblical view of missions?

> 1. Create an environment where missionaries can act normally (like you do).

Missionaries rarely feel that they can be natural or normal for fear of being looked upon as extravagant. So, most often they do not share felt needs, just needs that relate to the "missionary work" they were sent out to do. Send them some special care packages full of anything but the bare necessities to prime the pump of what they should expect on furlough.

> 2. Champion your missionaries on a corporate body level.

When local churches support a missionary and the pastor who was the missionary's champion moves on, the church often grows cold toward that missionary. The church body may not even know them, so support is often cut off leaving the foreign missionary in limbo, wondering if they should stay or return to their home.

> 3. Never cut missionary funds except for moral or theological infidelity.

Churches should have factors in place as part of their by-laws that guarantee that missionaries will be supported even when the pastor leaves, the church splits, etc. Additionally, the supporting church should have in place some type of support structure when there is a death in the family of the missionary and they need to travel, or if illness hits the missionary, or if the missionary retires, there are contingency plans in place.

Attitudes like this will require a major amount of time and wisdom vetting potential new missionaries, but every drop of sweat will be worth it. Our church policy is that we won't support a missionary unless he is elder qualified (according to 1 Timothy 3 and Titus 1) and is competent to occupy our pulpit on a Sunday morning.

4. Do not be chintzy supporters.

Forget the inadequate $25 per month support. Make it substantial. Your church should give enough monthly support to missionaries so that they visit you on furlough. Work toward giving 10% of your church budget to missionaries. Do not add more missionaries until your current "sent ones" are provided for sufficiently. Why not support some missionaries 100%?

5. Go for broke.

Spoil your missionaries. Go "above and beyond" serving them. Treat them like you would if your grandchildren came back from the field. Missionaries enjoy and appreciate nice things just like people at home do. They need a night out on occasion, a shopping trip, Christmas gifts, something other than clothes from the musty missionary barrel.

6. Always be hospitable.

Families in the church should be encouraged to invite missionaries to their homes for meals (without the pastor). Missionaries need to feel normal when they are on furlough. When your missionaries are on furlough the next time, ask them to stay at your house for their entire stay. Teach your children by actions what first-class love is. Provide the best food and the best accommodations you can as you serve those who serve well on the foreign field.

7. When the church staff receives raises, make sure the missionaries obtain the same amount.

8. Train up missionaries in your own church and send them out. This is a perfect way of guaranteeing the congregation knows who they are.

9. Don't ask missionaries for stories about snakes and wild mongoose attacks. The cross of Jesus Christ is dramatic enough.

10. Send your pastor and other short-term mission teams to help your missionaries (they have yummy breakfasts over there, cooked by maids).

11. Substitute "Pastors" for "Missionaries" and re-read this chapter.

Conclusion

When the visiting missionary leaves our church building after a weekend together ministering, what are our reactions? "It was good to see them." "The kids seemed pretty unruly." "I liked the jungle stories from our other missionary better." Would you volunteer to take them to the airport and then, after unloading their entire luggage cart at the airline departure terminal, cry like a newborn baby? Something very similar happened in the Bible. The Ephesian church understood missions. An endearing relationship with our missionaries is possible. Actually, it should be *normal*.

Paul called for the elders of Ephesus and gave them a biblical charge which ended this way:

> "In all things I have shown you that by working hard in this way we must help the weak and remember the words of the Lord Jesus, how he himself said, 'It is more blessed to give than to receive.'" And when he had said these things, he knelt down and prayed with them all. And there was much weeping on the part of all; they embraced Paul and kissed him, being sorrowful most of all because of the word he had spoken, that they would not see his face again. And they accompanied him to the ship. (Acts 20:35–38)

The idea of weeping and embracing a messenger of the gospel is surely a foretaste of heaven itself. United in purpose and "mission," both the senders and sent ones embrace until "death do us part." It is within the reach of every church and missionary!

Chapter Five

. . .

White Lie #5: Work Is Only a Means to an End (Work Is Strictly Secular)

. . .

Let's eavesdrop on two people sitting at their favorite coffee shop on a Monday morning. "How was your worship last week?" "Well, it was pretty good. We went to the church service, helped at the rest home dinner, and then we drove to the youth ministry outreach to assist in discipleship." "Now that is a nice answer and those are very good activities, but is that all you did for worship in the last seven days?" Insert perplexed look here. "Is that *all*?" "Well, what I was getting at is this: when I asked you the first question I really meant, 'Did you worship well at work last week?' My leading question was my deft way of trying to see if you rightly perceived your employment as worship. I have recently learned that whether you are a father who goes off to work every day, or a mother who literally wakes up at work every morning, work should be considered worship. I was shocked and encouraged to grasp that employment is not only a means to the end (getting wages to pay necessary bills), but it also must be viewed as the end in itself. In short, God cares about your motives and attitudes at work. God expects quality work. God expects that you treat work as a worshipful act unto Him. Work is worship."

Most people think too shortsightedly about work. Their thinking is myth-filled. Christians "work for the weekend." Believers "owe, so it's off to work they go." Saints scramble pell-mell for promotions and lucrative bonuses with stock options. No wonder most employees' job satisfaction rates are at an all-time low as they dolefully sing the pop tunes of the 1980s, "I don't like Mondays" or "Everybody's workin' for the weekend." Sadly, people who imbibe the mentality of these songs rarely "whistle while they work." There seem to be as many employment myths as there are hours in a workweek, including overtime. Sadly, the work fairytales stifle joy and job satisfaction. The average worker will experience around 4,000 Mondays in his or her life. That is a lot of days not to like. A farmer once quipped, "The hardest thing about milking cows is that they never stay milked." Not even on Monday. Can joy at work be experienced? Is job satisfaction a possibility? Read on and be ready for encouragement!

Let's examine some questions:

"Why do I work?"

"Should I like my work?"

"Does my employment really matter in light of eternity?"

"How can I have real job satisfaction?"

"Does work have to be royal drudgery?"

"Is working a necessary evil?"

"Construction" Points

The battle for godliness at work begins in the mind. Right thinking is imperative. One of my children was purposefully disobedient. I called the child into a private room for discipline. I began to ask a series of questions in an attempt to understand the faulty thought process so that I could be of help. "Why did you do that?" The response was epic: "I was not thinking right, Dad." Well, even though my child should have used the adverb "rightly" to modify "thinking," the child was absolutely correct and honest. Right thinking leads to right acting. Ideas have consequences. If you must know, I did not spank the child because the child personally owned the sin and gave such a classic answer fit for a future book project.

Let's examine seven thoughts about work that we will label as "construction" points. These are biblical thoughts designed for the reader to quickly construct a Christ-honoring worldview of employment so that you might think properly. May the Lord use these to transform work into true worship!

1. Before entering His public ministry, Jesus, the God-Man, was a carpenter.

Jesus rendered perfect obedience while He was on earth. The Eternal Son of God cloaked Himself with frail humanity and then lived a pure and spotless life on earth. The Bible teaches that Christ's motives were always clean and His actions were constantly holy. No matter how difficult the temptation was to bear, Jesus never succumbed to any sin of commission or omission. It is quite an accomplishment to say "no" to lying and lusting, but it is even more spectacular that Jesus always actively did His heavenly Father's will by saying, "yes" to righteousness. Simply, Jesus always loved the Lord His God with all His heart, soul, mind, and strength. Jesus never stopped loving His neighbor with a deep and abiding agape love. Never.

In the context of work and employment, Jesus was like other young men in the Hebrew culture in that He did what His father did for work. Specifically, Jesus learned the trade of a peasant because his earthly father was a carpenter. Scripture makes it clear that Jesus was both a carpenter and a son of a carpenter:

> "Is not this the carpenter, the son of Mary and brother of James and Joses and Judas and Simon? And are not his sisters here with us?" And they took offense at him. (Mark 6:3)

> "Is not this the carpenter's son? Is not his mother called Mary? And are not his brothers James and Joseph and Simon and Judas?" (Matthew 13:55)

Jesus was both a carpenter and a carpenter's son because Hebrew fathers regularly taught their sons their own trade so that a needed skill could be passed down to their sons. "Carpenter" in biblical Greek is *tekton*, which signifies a person who "works with his hands." Jesus and Joseph were men whose occupation was one of manual labor. Jesus' trade could be described as physically taxing, blue collar, and low on the social ladder's totem pole. Carpentry was not a trade for noblemen or princes. Amazingly, Jesus, the God-Man, was born in obscurity and humility. The Creator of the universe (Colossians 1:16–17) had poor parents and a birth that was clouded by controversy and shame. Jesus was a peasant. By today's understanding, Jesus got paid by the hour. Blue-collar.

Let us now consider what would be unimaginable for the rest of humanity—Jesus never sinned at work. Reread the last sentence. Jesus never sinned at work. Imagine the long hours and difficult working conditions of a poor carpenter's apprentice? Jesus even worked for a sinful boss, that is, his human stepfather, Joseph. I am sure Joseph was a wonderful father, but he was not perfect and he was not a boss without defects, failures, and sins. Yet, Jesus always obeyed His supervisor with joy. The Son of Man constantly had a good attitude during strenuous labor, without complaint, with a boss that was not like His heavenly Father. Jesus consistently honored His heavenly Father by His humble service to His earthly father. Jesus was the best worker ever.

If Jesus' life were only an example, we would both rejoice and cry simultaneously. Why? We would exalt in the fact that we have a true role model for employment, but we would weep because we could never live up to His perfection. Now get ready for the great news—because of the great doctrine of justification, God credits Christ's perfect obedience, including His obedience to His human boss, to all those who believe in the risen Jesus.

> For our sake he made him to be sin who knew no sin, so
> that in him we might become the righteousness of God.
> (2 Corinthians 5:21)

God looks at you and sees the righteous Christ even though you are not righteous. Specifically, God never sees you and your lack of obedience at work, because you are "in Christ." Are you beginning to whistle? Christ's perfect attitude at work is credited to every Christian.

2. Jesus accomplished the work of redemption.

The heavenly Father was pleased to send the Lord Jesus to save sinners. Jesus willingly agreed to go even though it was going to cost Him everything, including an excruciating death on the cross. Would anyone question the fact that Christ's life and work of redemption was work? Jesus labored. The Bible says,

> Jesus said to them, "My food is to do the will of him who
> sent me and to accomplish his work." (John 4:34)

> I glorified you on earth, having accomplished the work
> that you gave me to do. And now, Father, glorify me in
> your own presence with the glory that I had with you be-
> fore the world existed. (John 17:4–5)

Thankfully, Jesus did not fail at His work. Sweating in the Garden of Gethsemane and agonizingly dying on Calvary's tree was strenuous work, yet Jesus completed everything the Father gave Him to do. Jesus said, "It is finished," stating emphatically that the redemption was accomplished. Jesus worked for His earthly father and He worked for the glory of His heavenly Father as He accomplished our salvation. Jesus was the best worker who has ever lived. Work, therefore, is not beneath the dignity of a true human.

3. You are determined by who you are in Christ, not by your job title.

When people introduce themselves to one another, after they exchange names and appropriately firm handshakes, one of the two people inevitably asks, "What do you do for a living?" The question of employment is regularly seen as an efficient way to size up the status and perceived importance of the other individual. What if you are low on the status totem pole? What if your collar is blue? Whether Christians are garbage collectors or brain surgeons, the way God sees them transcends their employment status. Fundamentally, they are "in Christ." They are Christians before they are janitors or judges. Who you are is determined by your status in Christ, not by your job title or description.

> But now that faith has come, we are no longer under a guardian, for in Christ Jesus you are all sons of God, through faith. For as many of you as were baptized into Christ have put on Christ. There is neither Jew nor Greek, there is neither slave nor free, there is no male and female, for you are all one in Christ Jesus. (Galatians 3:25–28)

God sees you as a son or daughter before He sees you as a doctor, lawyer or a minimum wage earner. The Lord God recognizes you as a child of God before He notices you as soldier or milkman (do we have "milk people" any longer?). There is no room for pride if you are a prince, and there is no place for shame if you clean toilets. Your identity is found in the heavenly places in Christ Jesus.

I recently had my one-thousand-gallon septic tank drained and flushed. The man who was siphoning waste from the tank made a derogatory comment about his job. I told him that all honest work was God-honoring. He quickly deduced the fact that I was a pastor and then told me of his recent conversion. The worker was first a Christian. His identity was not only found in his smelly job. The man responded with joy. As he drove away, I distinctly heard something resembling whistling.

4. No secular/sacred bifurcations are allowed.

Most evangelical Christians erroneously believe that everything they do that relates to church is considered "sacred." They deem going to a worship service, serving the elderly at Bible studies, teaching Sunday school classes, and every other church-related activity as sacred or holy. So far, this line of thinking is accurate. The sticky wicket is in the converse. On the flip-side, the majority of folks believe their daytime job, exercise, and everything in-between, or outside of church, is "secular." Worship is certainly sacred, but everything a Christian does must be perceived within the rubric of sacred. Avoid the notion that "secular" means something that is not religious. The dictionary might say that "secular" involves a person thinking about life from a worldly perspective, but the Christian must see all of God's world, and everything in it, as belonging to God. The Dutch theologian Abraham Kuyper boomed in the conclusion of his message to inaugurate the Free University, "There is not a square inch in the whole domain of our human existence over which Christ, who is Sovereign over all, does not cry: 'Mine!'"[1]

Therefore, the Christian should jettison every concept about the secular/sacred bifurcation because it denies the Lordship of Jesus Christ over everything, especially employment. Take a minute to walk through the components of your life, especially focusing upon your job. Then agree with Jesus who says over every area, "Mine!" Ladies who stay home and work very hard at raising their children should be encouraged to know that the mundane and very repetitive dishes-and-diapers routine is not secular. Washing dishes to the glory of God? Yes! "Mine!"

Laymen who work either blue or white-collar jobs are doing God's ministry as much as those who have their collar on backwards (clergy). How refreshing it is to the soul to grasp the verity that *how* a 9–5 job is done actually matters to God. Martin Luther embraced such a truth:

> To call popes, bishops, priests, monks, and nuns, the religious class, but princes, lords, artizans [sic], and farm-workers the secular class, is a specious device...For all Christians

---

[1]Abraham Kuyper, "Sphere Sovereignty," in Abraham Kuyper: *A Centennial Reader*, ed. James D. Bratt (Grand Rapids, MI: Eerdmans, 1998), 488.

whatsoever really and truly belong to the religious class, and there is no difference among them except in so far as they do different work. . . . Hence we deduce that there is, at bottom, really no other difference between laymen, priests, princes, bishops ...between religious and secular, than that of office or occupation, and not that of Christian status.[2]

What you do at work matters for eternity. You can literally worship at work. The way you work directly reflects upon the Lordship of Christ. Your whole life is sacred. Nothing you do should be thought of as secular.

5. There will be work in heaven.

The notion of heaven being a place where fat cherubs strum harps and people float leisurely on puffy, fluffy clouds is not a biblical concept. Without a doubt, heaven will be heaven because we will be face to face with our Creator and Savior:

> And I heard a loud voice from the throne saying, "Behold, the dwelling place of God is with man. He will dwell with them, and they will be his people, and God himself will be with them as their God. He will wipe away every tear from their eyes, and death shall be no more, neither shall there be mourning, nor crying, nor pain anymore, for the former things have passed away." (Revelation 21:3–4)

But the Bible informs its readers that heaven will be a place where work is done. Adam was given work to do in the Garden of Eden before the Fall, and there is no reason to believe that in the eternal state there will not be work to be done. Stewardship over God's creation in the eternal state is certainly a possibility. The Bible does specifically teach that in heaven we will be "his servants" and that we "will reign":

> No longer will there be anything accursed, but the throne of God and of the Lamb will be in it, and his servants will worship him. They will see his face, and his name will be on their foreheads. And night will be no more. They will need no light of lamp or sun, for the Lord God will be their light, and they will reign forever and ever. (Revelation 22:3–5)

---

[2] "An Appeal to the Ruling Class," in John Dillenberger, ed., *Martin Luther: Selections from His Writings* (Garden City, NY: Anchor Books, 1961), 407, 409, 410.

The specifics of how we will serve and reign are not mentioned, but servants serve and rulers will have work to do. There will be no curse, so work will be a delightful and worshipful experience that we will actually enjoy doing. Can you imagine working for eternity without ever receiving a paycheck? Your work, service, and ruling will be out of gratitude for your Savior, the Lord Jesus Christ. Fat cherubs do not exist in heaven because they will be so busy serving the Lord that they will be in shape!

6. God expects faithfulness at work, not success.

There is so much pressure in the working world today. The corporate world is concerned about the bottom line and how that directly relates to stock holder dividends and monetary performance. For them, the bottom line is the bottom line. Sales quotas skyrocket while sales territories continue to shrink. Companies downsize, restructure, and are in a constant state of flux. Simultaneously, the world promotes the idea that success at work is the key to a happy and fulfilled life. Succeed or fail. Eat or be eaten. Is there any middle ground? Is there any sane ground? Thankfully, the answer is a resounding "yes!" God simply requires faithfulness. Nothing more. Nothing less. God sovereignly pushes people up corporate ladders and He demotes others according to His all-wise plan. God often gives human recognition for employment achievements, but He also decides that not everyone will be, by human standards, successful or profitable. God wants His children to be hardworking employees who leave their life and career in His faithful hands.

The pressure cooker of employment can be given immediate relief if Ephesians 2:10 is considered in the light of work. Paul wrote, "For we are his workmanship, created in Christ Jesus for good works, which God prepared beforehand, that we should walk in them." The Monday morning blahs can be transformed into joy when our minds grasp this truth and our hearts pray "Lord, help me to be faithful to walk in the good works you prepared beforehand for me today at work!" Can you hear the pressure being emancipated from that pressure cooker in office cubicles worldwide?

7. Work has value.

Besides providing a paycheck, work is intrinsically good and highly valued in the Bible:

> The LORD God took the man and put him in the garden of Eden to work it and keep it. (Genesis 2:15)

Go to the ant, O sluggard; consider her ways, and be wise. Without having any chief, officer, or ruler, she prepares her bread in summer and gathers her food in harvest. (Proverbs 6:6–8)

Additionally, employment keeps you out of trouble:

For even when we were with you, we would give you this command: If anyone is not willing to work, let him not eat. For we hear that some among you walk in idleness, not busy at work, but busybodies. Now such persons we command and encourage in the Lord Jesus Christ to do their work quietly and to earn their own living. (2 Thessalonians 3:10–12)

How to Work

Ephesians 6 presents the most convicting and compelling way a Christian should work:

Bondservants, obey your earthly masters with fear and trembling, with a sincere heart, as you would Christ, not by the way of eye-service, as people-pleasers, but as bondservants of Christ, doing the will of God from the heart, rendering service with a good will as to the Lord and not to man, knowing that whatever good anyone does, this he will receive back from the Lord, whether he is a bondservant or is free. (Ephesians 6:5–8)

Paul dictates the proper attitude of obedience that God requires for all workers, slave or free:

- Obey with fear and trembling (language signifying the relationship of subordination).
- Obey with single-mindedness.
- Obey even when people are not looking.
- Obey with good will.
- Obey with great expectation (a reward from the Lord).

If first-century slaves were required to work for their masters with these attitudes, how much more should twenty-first-century Christians strive to work without complaint?

Conclusion

A right and biblical view of work helps balm the irritation of low wages, job insecurity, boredom, and difficulty. May God grant you the attitude of Br'er Rabbit when you work, "makin' a dollar a minute." But more than that, may God grant you motivation to really work for the glory of Jesus Christ, so that Christ's fame will increase through you. Whistle away.

Chapter Six

. . .

White Lie #6: The Focus is on the Family

. . .

In Christian circles, thanks to an extremely popular radio show, almost everyone could fill in the following blank properly: "Focus on the _____." The answer is, of course, "Focus on the *Family*." While the family is under obvious attack in our generation and needs all the encouragement it can receive, the radio show would actually be more biblical if the name was, "Focus on the Family Serving Jesus Christ." The family is not the terminal focus for the Christian. As important and wonderful as the family is for a Christian parent, child, or church, the family is a divine institution given for greater purposes than the family itself.

No one doubts that the family is bombarded and attacked by secular and anti-religious media, educational hierarchies, and various institutions. Certainly, the mastermind, Satan, is behind the well-planned carpet-bombing approach in an attempt to destroy the family. Since the Lord restrains sin through the government, church, and family, it is no wonder that the Adversary does everything in his power to thwart the purpose and plan of God as he launches missiles at each of God's restraining entities.

From another perspective, unbelievers regularly focus on the family. Mormons focus on the family. Decent citizens value the family. Buddhists love the family and deem it important. While exceptions to these examples will be numerous, the point still remains valid—there is nothing particularly Christian about focusing on the family. Therefore, the real question concerning the purpose of the family must recognize the reason for the family's existence and the family's relationship to the Lord Jesus Christ.

Lest anyone misunderstand, the protection of the family is a non-negotiable. The family needs guarding, prayer, and shielding from hostile, external forces. This chapter attempts to push the theological envelope by underscoring how the family needs protection from making itself the be-all and end-all. In other words, the focus must never be on the family alone (I am sure that the radio show, "Focus on the Family," would agree, but their name lends itself to wrong thinking). Christ must be the focus of every church, every person, and every family. When the family focuses upon the Lord of the church, then everything is seen properly and put in its rightful place, including the family.

Put another way, even if the focus was completely and fully on the family, there is more to do. The family can and should be viewed as important, valuable, God-given, and wonderful, but it must not receive undue focus and concentration as the final consideration. Rather, the family is God's gracious work of love, perfectly designed to promote His agenda through His Son, the Lord Jesus Christ.

Let's examine the importance of the family, the origin of family, why the family must focus on Jesus Christ, and then offer some concluding thoughts and some "take aways," particularly designed to stir the reader to action in light of the truth presented—that the focus of the family needs to be upward to the Lord and away from itself.

The Family's Place

The family's significance must not be undervalued, especially since the family unit is not only God's idea but also it is the Lord's sphere of abounding blessing. Psalm 128 highlights what the Sovereign Lord thinks about the family:

> Blessed is everyone who fears the LORD, who walks in his ways! You shall eat the fruit of the labor of your hands; you shall be blessed, and it shall be well with you. Your wife will be like a fruitful vine within your house; your children will be like olive shoots around your table. Behold, thus shall the man be blessed who fears the LORD. The LORD bless you from Zion! May you see the prosperity of Jerusalem all the days of your life! May you see your children's children! Peace be upon Israel!

God abundantly blesses His children with families of their own. The refrain in Psalm 128 is "blessed." Sinful people deserve curses from a thrice-holy God, but God is gracious, longsuffering, and good. He blesses. He gives. The psalmist declares that a husband's wife is a great reward and, in addition, the children are gracious trimmings to the family unit. The problem occurs when people do not think properly about Psalm 128. The Holy Spirit did not intend for the readers of Psalm 128 to understand that the family was an end in and of itself. God designed the family unit for a purpose, and that purpose is outwardly focused (or better yet, "upwardly" focused). In other words, as wonderful as the family is, it is not the end or terminal focus.

A very common marriage foible occurs when the husband and wife concentrate on their marriage too much. How can that be a problem? Answer: the marriage is not the end—it is the means to something bigger and greater than the marriage itself. Marriages were designed by God to give Him glory. Weddings inaugurate the launching pad for two people committed to each other in a holy covenant, determined, by the grace of God, to give themselves to each other so that their marriage might give itself to the praise of its Maker. When married couples forget this fact mentally and it manifests itself in the inner workings of their relationship, God graciously allows the couple to experience the fruit of the error of building their marriage on their marriage. Strife, impasse, and dissatisfaction often occur.

A wife cannot be her husband's ultimate "need-meeter" and absolute "desire-fulfiller." A married man quickly realizes that the woman of his dreams cannot literally fulfill all of his dreams, hopes, and aspirations. The problem is not with his wife—it is with the husband's false notions of marriage and marriage's purpose. Similarly, married ladies come face to face with reality when they grasp the cold, hard fact that their husbands are not equipped to give them everything their hearts long for and need in this world. Counter intuitively, all this sober realization is a very, very good wake-up call. God works through the pain, suffering, disappointment, and heartache of a marriage built upon itself. God then has the full attention of the married couple. Marital bliss is still obtainable, but it is not found within the marriage itself. Marital satisfaction and happiness begins by remembering why they married each other in the first place, that is, to serve Jesus Christ and His church. Originally, the couple both recognized that they could better serve their Savior as a married couple than as single people.

Maybe it is not perfectly fair to call a marriage built on itself "cannibalistic," but since this is my book, I will use that word for effect. The same holds true for any person in the world: focus on self and the wheels of life fall off. When anyone loves themselves with all their heart, soul, mind, and strength, bad things happen and horrible emotions are experienced. Why does God allow such pain? God gets our attention as He lovingly disciplines us for our selfish behavior. When someone touches the hot stove and gets a blister-forming burn, they do not yelp, "God, I am mad at you for giving me nerve endings at the tips of my fingers!" It is the goodness and grace of God to warn us, through nerves and pain sensors, of impending trouble and immediate danger. Pain motivates. Christian couples should be on the lookout for the pain that occurs when marriages are too ingrown so that they may repent of serving themselves and focus together upon serving their Lord and Master.

By biblical definition, marriages, with or without children, constitute a "family." A family is a husband and a wife, whether they have children or not. In either case, the family should focus on the Lord Jesus and His church. Families, with fathers taking lead, should respond to their great salvation by serving God and their neighbors out of hearts filled with gratitude.

God Delegates the Stewardship of Children He Has Created

Is possession or ownership nine tenths (or nine points) of the law? The common expression, derived from the Scots, "possession is eleven points in the law, and they say there are but twelve," touts that it is easier to keep your possessions than it is to take them from someone else. If people argue about property, the person in possession of the land or goods is presumably the rightful owner, unless there is testament to the contrary. While the government recognizes that parents are the legal guardians of their children (whether naturally born or adopted), parents need to remember who ultimately "owns" their children. Parents do not actually "possess" their children. The testimony of DNA does not overthrow God's fundamental ownership. The infamous Hatfield-McCoy quarrel centered on Floyd Hatfield's possession of pigs that the McCoys declared as their swine. Squatters' rights might have won the American Wild West, but God Almighty gives no credence to fathers and mothers homesteading children. God owns every child. Parents are simply stewards of God's creation.

The Bible regularly describes children with the refrain, "given by

God." Saints in the Old Testament had regular reminders to help them recognize God's graciousness in giving them children:

> Behold, I and the children whom the LORD has given me are signs and portents in Israel from the LORD of hosts, who dwells on Mount Zion. (Isaiah 8:18)

When Israel saw Joseph's sons, he said,

> "Who are these?" Joseph said to his father, "They are my sons, whom God has given me here." And he said, "Bring them to me, please, that I may bless them." (Genesis 48:8–9)

> Behold, children are a heritage from the LORD, the fruit of the womb a reward. (Psalm 127:3)

Children are a direct gift from an all-loving God. Therefore, every son and daughter is on loan! Every parent will answer to their Creator for the eighteen years (on average) they cared for the children God gave them. Children are great blessings, but they are also trusts from the Lord. Some people view children as rug rats, better seen than heard, snot-nosed brats, or worse! The Scriptural position assesses children as gifts from God, temporally on loan.

Parents with older children realize the brevity of their "ownership," especially as the college and marriage years zoom toward them at what seems like the speed of light. Empty nests are reminders of the fact that parents do not own their children; rather, the dads and moms are only stewards of what the Lord graciously and sovereignly entrusted to their care for a season. Paul stated, in a different context, "For who sees anything different in you? What do you have that you did not receive? If then you received it, why do you boast as if you did not receive it?" (1 Corinthians 4:7). The complete family will not always be in place, so live in light of your children walking out of the house spiritually mature enough to be a Christian adult.

Families Should Focus on Jesus Christ

Every family, specifically the husband and wife, preaches something about the relationship Jesus has with His church. Read carefully Ephesians 5:22–33 with an eye toward the greater reality Paul highlights:

Wives, submit to your own husbands, as to the Lord. For the husband is the head of the wife even as Christ is the head of the church, his body, and is himself its Savior. Now as the church submits to Christ, so also wives should submit in everything to their husbands. Husbands, love your wives, as Christ loved the church and gave himself up for her, that he might sanctify her, having cleansed her by the washing of water with the word, so that he might present the church to himself in splendor, without spot or wrinkle or any such thing, that she might be holy and without blemish. In the same way husbands should love their wives as their own bodies. He who loves his wife loves himself. For no one ever hated his own flesh, but nourishes and cherishes it, just as Christ does the church, because we are members of his body. "Therefore a man shall leave his father and mother and hold fast to his wife, and the two shall become one flesh." *This mystery is profound, and I am saying that it refers to Christ and the church.* However, let each one of you love his wife as himself, and let the wife see that she respects her husband (emphasis added).

The husband preaches, by his actions toward his wife, a living sermon of how the Lord Jesus loves His church. Likewise, but conversely, the wife proclaims by her actions toward her husband how the church submits to Jesus Christ. New England pastor, Jonathan Edwards (1703–1758), echoed the ramifications of Ephesians 5 for every member of the family, saying, "Every Christian family ought to be as it were a little church, consecrated to Christ, and wholly influenced and governed by his rules."[1]

If the family focuses on themselves, their children's manners, successes, or achievements, the family misses the ultimate goal for the family and the husband's life-sermon falls short of the exaltation of Jesus Christ. Every family needs to have a gospel-oriented goal and purpose. Exalting God's glory must be the priority. Parents should certainly strive to teach their children manners and proper behavior, but there is a greater goal—the exaltation of Jesus in the lives of every parent and child. Farley understands the role of salvation in the life of the family:

---

[1] Jonathan Edwards, *A Farewell Sermon* (Minneapolis, MN: Curiosmith, 2011), 56.

Their children will live forever. This is a staggering thought. We cannot imagine "forever." Nevertheless, the destiny of our children either will be love that surpasses knowledge, joy inexpressible and full of glory, coupled with peace that passes understanding, or it will be weeping, wailing, and gnashing of teeth. There is no middle ground. Therefore, the Christian does not parent for this life only. The believing parent labors to prepare each child for the day of judgment. The stakes are inexpressibly high.[2]

Conclusion

Many people today take slogans or radio jingles (in this case, radio show titles) and make them their primary doctrine, which then drives their behavior. Christians, because of everything that Jesus has done for them, must strive to focus their family on the Eternal Son. The Bible, not successful radio ministries, should set the course for the family.

Response

1. Schedule family vacations at a Christian camp or retreat center. Many families spend thousands at secular resorts or theme parks (there is nothing wrong with those choices), but they rarely consider family camps that center on the Word of God and Christ the Son.

2. Pray that God would make your house the most popular house in the neighborhood. Unbelieving children are drawn to homes where the love of Christ is valued and shown.

3. Have fun with your kids. Christians should have the most fun and the most joy. They worship a sovereign and good God who grants much fruit through His Holy Spirit, including joy.

4. Dads must lead. Vacuums of leadership will certainly be filled. When a father abdicates his God-ordained leadership because of laziness or busyness, bad things will happen in a family. A well-known feminist leader disdainfully said, "Fathers are a biological necessity, but a psychological absurdity." On the contrary, Christian leader William P. Farley reflects God's perspective saying, "The common denominator between success and failure seems to be the spiritual depth and sincerity of the parents, especially

---

[2]William P. Farley, *Gospel-Powered Parenting* (Phillipsburg: P & R Publishing, 2009), 41.

the spiritual depth and sincerity of the father. There seems to be a strong correlation between the faith, commitment, and sincerity of the family head and the spiritual vitality of his adult children."[3]

5. Fathers, read through Proverbs and underline every time the author says, "my son," or its equivalent. Here is a sampling, which underlines the father's role in teaching and leading his children (these proverbs are from the NASB translation):

1:8—Hear, my son, your father's instruction and do not forsake your mother's teaching.

2:1—My son, if you will receive my words and treasure my commandments within you...

3:1—My son, do not forget my teaching, but let your heart keep my commandments.

4:10—Hear, my son, and accept my sayings and the years of your life will be many.

5:1—My son, give attention to my wisdom, incline your ear to my understanding.

6:1—My son, if you have become surety for your neighbor, if you have given a pledge for a stranger...

7:1—My son, keep my words and treasure my commandments within you.

19:27—Cease listening, my son, to discipline, and you will stray from the words of knowledge.

23:15—My son, if your heart is wise, my own heart also will be glad.

24:21—My son, fear the LORD and the king; do not associate with those who are given to change.

27:11—Be wise, my son, and make my heart glad, that I may reply to him who reproaches me.

---

[3]Ibid., 15.

Chapter Seven

White Lie #7: Bodily Exercise Does Not Profit

The myth of the governance of the physical body is over this veritable cage-match verse:

> for while bodily training is of some value, godliness is of value in every way, as it holds promise for the present life and also for the life to come. (1 Timothy 4:8)

How does a person interpret the verse above? Usually, "fitness herme-neutics" determine how 1 Timothy 4:8 is understood and then "worked out" (pun intended). If a person is fit, in shape, or trim (or something close), they will put emphasis on the word "value" in "bodily training is of some *value*." Conversely, if a person rarely works out, is overweight, and the first number of their BMI (Body Mass Index) starts with a 2 or 3, then they will put the emphasis on the word "some" in "bodily training is of *some* value." Try saying the verse out loud with the different words emphasized. See what I mean? To use the language of King James, who was said to be a little paunchy himself, "For exercise of the body profiteth a little." "Profiteth" or "little"? Christians need to "weigh in" with the truth contained in the Bible, especially as it relates to the world's modern obsession, that is, the body.

"Body Building"

Believers are incessantly assaulted with a variety of worldly views and media perspectives, each vying for preeminence in the hearts and minds of Bible-toting Christians. Every follower of Christ agrees that they must avoid pagan thoughts about their "body" and "build" a Christian worldview. The essence of every erroneous worldview of the body can be distilled into a few ancient, yet still relevant, views: the Stoics taught the body was the dungeon of the soul; Epicureans believed the body was pleasure's tool; the Greeks worshiped the body. Each ancient view has its modern adherents, even though many of the followers would not be able to recognize the foundational philosophies or pronounce the names. Christians must resist the force of unbiblical viewpoints and come face to face with the reality that their bodies belong to God, their Creator. What one believes determines how one acts. Theology determines methodology. Right thinking about the body will inevitably lead to treating the body as God desires.

How should a Christian view the body in the context of sex? In 1 Corinthians 6, Paul systematically walks the carnal Corinthians through the logic of physical purity:

> "Food is meant for the stomach and the stomach for food"—and God will destroy both one and the other. The body is not meant for sexual immorality, but for the Lord, and the Lord for the body. And God raised the Lord and will also raise us up by his power. Do you not know that your bodies are members of Christ? Shall I then take the members of Christ and make them members of a prostitute? Never! Or do you not know that he who is joined to a prostitute becomes one body with her? For, as it is written, "The two will become one flesh." But he who is joined to the Lord becomes one spirit with him. Flee from sexual immorality. Every other sin a person commits is outside the body, but the sexually immoral person sins against his own body. Or do you not know that your body is a temple of the Holy Spirit within you, whom you have from God? You are not your own, for you were bought with a price. So glorify God in your body. (1 Corinthians 6:13–20)

The apostle's immediate concern was how the Corinthians viewed the use of their bodies sexually. Ancient Corinth was a port city known for moral turpitude and sexual vices. Paul's heart yearns for his readers to embrace a biblical view of their bodies so that they will honor the Lord Jesus and simultaneously run from the sin that grossly dominated their lives as unbelievers. Even though the context of 1 Corinthians 6 is the relationship between sexual purity and the body, there are many principles which can be directly applied to the context of the body, working out, fitness, and how these relate to godliness.

At the building block or foundational level, Paul's exhortation reveals five valuable truths, which serve as a scaffolding for the Christian to properly view their body. First, the body should be cared for because God owns every person's body. God created the physical body as the instrument of serving Him (1 Corinthians 6:13). Second, the body will one day be raised by God's power; therefore, one must be careful with their body. God will glorify the Christian's body, yet it will still remain the person's body (1 Corinthians 6:14). Therefore, it would be shortsighted to abuse or neglect the body. Third, the physical bodies of all Christians are members of Christ (1 Corinthians 6:15–17). Fourth, believers' bodies are the temple of the Holy Spirit (1 Corinthians 6:19). Fifth, Christ has paid the purchase price for the body (1 Corinthians 6:20). The combination of all five truths helps reinforce each particular truth so that every reader can grasp Paul's point—the body matters to God, so it must matter to every Christian.

God actually owns your body: from the top of your head to the tip of your toes. Christ's redemption of believers' bodies was accomplished with the ransom price of His own blood. Slave trafficking was rampant in Corinth, so the Corinthians easily comprehended the ramifications of ransom and ownership. A holy God purchased unholy people with a holy ransom, and the response must be holy living with, and in, the body given to each Christian. Paul drove home the point that sexual sin was unacceptable because it involved using the body. Bodies must glorify God.

Context Profiteth Much

The verse that started the debate, and the chapter, has a context. The verses before and after 1 Timothy 4:8 assist the Bible reader's apprehension and interpretation:

> If you put these things before the brothers, you will be a
> good servant of Christ Jesus, being trained in the words of
> the faith and of the good doctrine that you have followed.
> Have nothing to do with irreverent, silly myths. Rather
> train yourself for godliness; for while bodily training is of
> some value, godliness is of value in every way, as it holds
> promise for the present life and also for the life to come.

The saying is trustworthy and deserving of full acceptance. For to this end we toil and strive, because we have our hope set on the living God, who is the Savior of all people, especially of those who believe. (1 Timothy 4:6–10)

Earlier in 1 Timothy, Paul was instructing his legate Timothy through a variety of topics which all related to leading Christ's church. Now Paul pushes Timothy to live out the doctrine that he has just been taught. Bodily training has some usefulness. It is beneficial for life on the earth. But the advantage of every drop of sweat through physical training ends at the grave. There is something that yields a greater return on investment—training in godliness. Paul demonstrates a parallel between the partial benefit of bodily exercise and the full compensation for godliness. Paul holds the essential nature of godliness before Timothy's eyes. Godliness, a sincere piety toward God, is essential for every Christian leader and every Christian.

Just as spirited exertion is needed for an athlete's disciplined life, spiritual exercise, or growth in godliness, is mandatory. Paul employs athletic metaphors to boost his argument with the spiritual equivalent of a caffeine-boosted protein shake. "Train" could be translated "exercise." Athletes go all out for their competitions and so should Christian pastors. Labor. Strive. Sweat. Toil. Work out. Eat well. Spiritually strive and stretch. Instead of guzzling creatine drinks, Christians need to imbibe nourishment from God's Word. Pastors should avoid godless myths just as much as body builders distance themselves from chili fries with fake cheese sauce. Fitness in the current life is valuable, but godliness has a value in the present life and in eternity.

Beauty and Vanity

Most readers could finish the first part of this verse, "Charm is deceitful, and beauty is _____." What word is missing? If you said "vain," then you are correct. But can you remember the rest of the verse? Proverbs 31:30 says, "Charm is deceitful, and beauty is vain, but a woman who fears the LORD is to be praised" (The NASB and KJV also translate Proverbs 31:30 with "vain.") Is beauty really vain? Just a few moments of contemplation should disavow anyone from such thinking. Anyone who says, "beauty is vain," is either ugly (handsomely challenged), married to someone who is more rich than beautiful, or they have not seen my wife or three daughters. The Hebrew word for "beauty" actually describes someone's bodily shape or the symmetry of his or her features. Elegance would be an apt idea for the Hebrew word used here for "beauty." When men see women, God has designed the man to notice the beauty of the woman, especially his wife. Who would argue that such a sight is "vain?" Remember your wedding? Was your wife's beauty vain on that day? In that dress? On that night?

While beauty is not vain, it certainly is fleeting or transient. The Hebrew word for "vain" is *hebel*, which literally means, "vapor." Beauty is nice while it lasts, but King Lemuel is saying that beauty disappears. In light of the temporary nature of beauty, women who fear the Lord are to be praised since this virtue remains when the wrinkles deepen. Here today, gone tomorrow. Beauty is vain if vanity considers its temporary nature. The NIV (1984) properly renders Proverbs 31:30, "Charm is deceptive, and beauty is fleeting; but a woman who fears the LORD is to be praised." Women might be "easy on the eye" when they are young- er, but age inevitably catches up with them and so do the wrinkles, gray hair, and inverted hour glass figure that is best described by using "car- nival mirror" terminology. As men age, they acquire paunchy stomachs, baldness caps their heads, and hair begins to sprout just about every- where else. Fleeting. Enough about the men, because the passage we are discussing deals with women—thankfully! Beauty is not vain, it just, as the New Living Bible states, "does not last." A lesser-known Bible version, God's Word Translation, is even picturesque in its description, quipping, "beauty evaporates." The writer of Proverbs 31 wants every reader to measure the value of a wife on the enduring qualities that have their focus upon the LORD. Beauty does fade, but godliness lasts. There is permanent and long-term value in a lady who fears the LORD. Paul's point in 1 Timothy 4:8 resembles Proverbs 31:30 in the fact that some things have value (exercise and beauty), but the real attention must be upon the things with the greater value (godliness and fearing the LORD). Think "good, better, best."

Old Testament Diets

Diets and nutritional programs founded upon Old Testament dietary laws intended for Israel have been multiplying like rabbits in springtime. Run from them as fast as you did from those new-fangled potato chips introduced in the early 1990s containing a secret sauce. Frito Lay made chips with a fat substitute that had no added fat, calories, or cholester- ol. Olestra was marketed under the "WOW brand," but the real "wow" factor was the FDA mandated label on the back, which warned, "This Product Contains Olestra. Olestra may cause abdominal cramping and loose stools. Olestra inhibits the absorption of some vitamins and other nutrients. Vitamins A, D, E and K have been added." In other words, these potato chips cause steatorrhea. Propriety prevents a description of that word, but any word ending in "-orrhea" telegraphs its meaning. Look it up on Google, if you dare. It is not certain that diets based on Mosaic Law will produce "-orrhea," but it is certain that you will have to produce your wallet in order to acquire the book. I wish I could slap a warning label on the back of every diet book based on the Old Testament with the words:

> Now the Spirit expressly says that in later times some will depart from the faith by devoting themselves to deceitful spirits and teachings of demons, through the insincerity of liars whose consciences are seared, who forbid marriage and require abstinence from foods that God created to be received with thanksgiving by those who believe and know the truth. For everything created by God is good, and nothing is to be rejected if it is received with thanksgiving, for it is made holy by the word of God and prayer. (1 Timothy 4:1–5)

There is no "Christian" view of dieting per se, so please be careful not to label something that God has declared good as bad. When it comes to food, Christians need to center on the "how much," not the "what." 1 Timothy 4:1–5 has forever nixed the "what" issue. Eat what you like. Christians are not under Mosaic Law. Christians can eat whatever they choose to eat. If a believer wants to be a vegan, he or she can, but it does not make the person more holy or obedient to God. Vegetarians, by choice or conviction, have no biblical support for their choice. Rather, it is simply a decision based upon nutrition, propaganda, preference, or listening to Ellen G. White. Human omnivores can freely decide to be herbivores if they so choose, but again, their choice has nothing to do with being godlier or more holy. If the goal is to maintain weight or to lose weight, caloric intake is the key to unlock the weight issue. Do not fall for the error that concludes some foods (Old Testament) are spiritually or physically better because "they are in the Bible." Caloric intake is directly related to a person's self control, which is part of the fruit of the Holy Spirit in the believer's life:

> But the fruit of the Spirit is love, joy, peace, patience, kindness, goodness, faithfulness, gentleness, *self-control*; against such things there is no law. And those who belong

to Christ Jesus have crucified the flesh with its passions and desires. (Galatians 5:22–24, emphasis added)

Underdoing or Overdoing or Just Right

The physical body is regularly underemphasized or overemphasized by Christians. If the biblical view is when the clock's long hand is on the 6, then it is easy for sinful, finite humans to sway to 7 or veer off to 5. Put another way, Christians, in their search to please the Lord at a biblical 6 often oscillate between underemphasizing the body by neglect and overemphasizing it by worship and undue attention. Like pseudo-pagans, Christians can fall into treating their bodies in a mystical manner. A Platonic hangover fleshes itself out by viewing the body as fleshy, fleshly, or like a sort of Christian rental car. How long does it take the average rental car driver to floor the accelerator as they drive out of the airport rental car bay? The body needs care because whatever we do for the Lord is done in our bodies. Your body matters.

Neither does the body need the equivalent of a daily royal spa treatment. It does not take much imagination to visualize believers rubbing, scrubbing, and over-exfoliating their bodies. All too often, Christians can buy into Hollywood's obsession with thinness, beauty, and body idolatry. Now there certainly are readers who don't "under do" physical exercise, rather, they, like the author himself, tend toward "over doing it." An inordinate focus on the temporal and perishing is a sign of spiritual immaturity. Bodily exercise is profitable, but an excess of exercise, especially at the expense of working out your salvation with fear and trembling (Philippians 2:12), is more than unprofitable, it is anti-profitable. Maybe a good rule of thumb should be: make sure more time is spent in God's Word than in Gold's Gym.

The Greek world in the New Testament times was dominated by the worship and adoration of beauty, whether it was the body, literature or architecture. The physical body's place of sculpting was called the *gumnasia*, or gymnasium. Make sure you avoid the modern-day equivalent, namely plastic surgery for cosmetic purposes, diet obsessions, and the infernal quest for a perfect, thin body. While many Christians today do not inject anabolic steroids, they can be just as obsessed by body image and the quest for something different than they have.

Working Out and Holy Ghost Praise-aerobics

I love working out with weights. Long bike rides make me happy. Walking is fun. Since my bad lower back no longer affords me the ability to jog, I now concur with Dwight Pentecost that jogging, for most people, should be better termed "jiggling." Besides burning calories, physical activity helps people sleep better at night, allows time for meaningful conversations, and increases stamina for life. Wisdom demands a healthy dose of exercise. If you would like to have more stamina and energy for the ministry of the Lord Jesus Christ and His church, then some exercise is in order. I know that my database of knowledge in this area is far from empirical; it is my experience that the majority of Christians could use some more physical activity. Listen to good preaching on your iPod while you work out. Go on a bike ride with your child. Swim with your wife. There are a myriad of activities that can be done with other Christians. You can even choose exercises that take place outside, so that the beauty of God's creation can be contemplated as you benefit from the exercise.

The most motivating reason to exercise is the advancement of the gospel. Hone your body for the sake of the kingdom. Flabby, short-breathed Christians have zero stamina. Since Christians are in a race for their Lord, run! Paul wrote:

> Do you not know that in a race all the runners run, but only one receives the prize? So run that you may obtain it. Every athlete exercises self-control in all things. They do it to receive a perishable wreath, but we an imperishable. So I do not run aimlessly; I do not box as one beating the air. But I discipline my body and keep it under control, lest after preaching to others I myself should be disqualified. (1 Corinthians 9:24–27)

Paul was no stranger to athletic games, and he regularly employed athletic metaphors to drive home spiritual points. In this passage, Paul pushes his readers to understand his all-consuming desire to propagate the gospel of Jesus Christ. "Single-mindedness" summarizes excellent racers in either the Isthmian or Olympic games, and it must characterize gospel workers. Self-discipline is also mandatory for athletes and preachers. Hardship during training yields the fruit of reward later. To punish one's body would be ludicrous if there was no possible payoff at the end of the race or apostolic mission. Like Paul, race to win the Christian life. While 1 Corinthians 9:24–27 does not directly encourage physical exercise, it certainly does not condemn it.

Paul uses a familiar rhetorical device, arguing from the lesser to the greater. For every Christian, ministry is like running. Ministry requires self-control. Ministry necessitates discipline. Isn't it difficult to be laborious in ministry while simultaneously out of shape? Isaac Watts penned, "Must I be carried to the skies on flowery beds of ease, while others fought to win the prize and sailed through bloody seas?" Christians have something before them that is so much more valuable than a victor's crown, which in Paul's day was often made out of withered celery stalks. Yum. Can't spiritual self-discipline and self-denial be helped by a body that can withstand a lack of sleep, hardships, and turmoil? 1 Corinthians 9:27 describes Paul disciplining his body for ministry. Literally, the Greek word for "discipline" is "to hit under the eye" or "to bruise the eye." The apostle gives himself a figurative black eye as he boxes himself. Far from actual flagellation, Paul uses imagery to point to an important truth—he wants to show the rigorous nature of apostolic ministry. Ask the question of yourself, "Am I overtired because I am not taking care of my body like I should?"

Conclusion

Bodily exercise is important for the Christian and it is profitable, but there is something more important, that is, spiritual exercise, or what Paul terms, "godliness."

Response

1. Is food your functional idol? Does food give the comfort, pleasure, and fulfillment that should be found in your Lord and Savior Jesus Christ?

2. Is exercise mandatory for your day to go well?

3. Can a Christian be physically lazy and undisciplined yet be spiritual disciplined? Why, or why not?

4. Is fat killing more Baptists than alcohol is killing Presbyterians?

5. Are obesity and gluttony the same thing?

6. Does the humanity of Jesus help reinforce the need for a Christian's stewardship of his or her body?

7. Does the fact that you will receive a resurrected body have any impact on how you take care of your body on earth?

8. Aren't you glad you have a Savior who saves from sin so completely that there will no vestiges of sin in heaven, including those sins that you committed with your body on earth?

9. Is it more important to go to the gym or to read the Bible? Can you read your Bible at the gym?

10. Are you willing to make strenuous sacrifices for the Kingdom of God? Similar to what marathon runners sacrifice as they train?

11. What is the context of Ezekiel 4? Are you sure you want to eat judgment bread?

Chapter Eight

, , ,

White Lie #8: Green Is God's Favorite Color

, , ,

A United Methodist church in Plano, Texas bragged about creating a veritable buzz around town. With what, you ask? How? The answer lies in their new-fangled urinals. The Associate Pastor, Reverend Alexandra (her last name is withheld to protect the guilty), boldly proclaimed, "Everyone wants to know what the waterless urinals are like." Church growth at its finest, I guess? Yes, but if more people begin to attend this church because they have famous über-urinals, won't that actually cause the low flow plumbing to be used more often? I digress. The same church also touted their new pipe organ, which was installed with special eco-friendly adhesives and sealants. I wonder if it still sounds organ-y? But wait, there is more. If you travel in an energy-efficient car or ride a bike to church, you get a sweet parking spot near the front of their building. I have to wonder, if you were that into eco-friendly concepts, shouldn't you park in the very back so that you could walk farther, thus emitting, by your breathing, more carbon dioxide for the flora and fauna? Are activities like those at this Plano church really demonstrating good stewardship of God's resources? When a church's claim to fame is low-flow toilets and waterless urinals, don't they have a serious problem in terms of Christ's Great Commission (Matthew 28:18–20)? Yes, they do.

Green Churches are hot, errr, popular, these days. One internet site exclaims, "In the Book of Revelation, John describes a great 'tree of life' and declares that the 'leaves of the tree will be for the healing of the nations.' To address the planetary emergency presented by climate change, all 'nations'—and yes, denomi-Nations—must find ways to work together. For most faith communities, our buildings present the best opportunity to make a real difference." No wonder John Calvin never wrote a commentary on Revelation. Now it all makes sense, or does it? Should churches become more environmentally friendly with healthy "toxic-free sacred spaces," trendy geothermal heating systems, and "Earth Care" immersion programs? Maybe the Green version of the Great Commission could be "reduce, reuse, recycle, and lo, the Green Church Initiative is with you, even to the end of carbon pollutants." Well, I guess it is not so great, and it is a pretty poor commission.

Even if you think that I have chosen some extreme examples of ecclesiastical green power, there is no doubt that Christians everywhere are tuned into being aware of taking care of the environment and many are now considering how to "green" their church buildings, parking lots and local church ecosystems. How biblical is the overall "green" philosophy? Does God care about the environment? Did Jesus mandate His own version of "Earth Day?" What should churches and Christians do? How should Christians navigate the global promotion of taking care of the earth, water, and air? Can the church learn from Greenpeace? Did the Reformation overlook the importance of the environment? Read on with all the bravery of a Greenpeace volunteer who is shackled to a whaling boat.

The outline for this chapter is simple. State the myth. Support the stated myth. No, that would not make sense since a myth cannot be supported. Let's try again: state the myth and then support why the myth is lore.

What is the overarching fable in this chapter? Simply, the myth is that God actually desires His church to spend time, money, and resources on "green" initiatives. Put another way, God is not green. Green programs are low on God's priority list, so they should be low on the totem pole of your "to-do" lists.

The Agenda

Most Americans have heard of Earth Day, which was originally designed to celebrate the earth and bolster mindfulness of the natural environment. Since its inception, Earth Day has spawned several spin-offs including a United Nations version entitled International Mother Earth Day. Most people today know more than they want to know about Earth Day. The green movement has excelled in spreading their gospel, lo, even to the ends of the earth. Simultaneously, it seems the church is losing her moorings, often unsure of the purpose of her existence. Eco-activism-fueled environmentalism-awareness education pushes itself onto every major political and media-driven platform. Green people are good at getting out their agenda, and the church often teeter-totters between ecclesiastical and environmental agendas.

I never acquired a taste for the Earth Day ecology flag. It reminded me too much of the Oregon Duck's football logo plastered on their less-than-fierce-looking helmets. Maybe the eerie similarity is more than coincidental after all? It probably was planned on purpose, knowing Oregon's penchant for the environment. Not to be outdone by the flag, Earth Day needed a psalm to rally and unite, so the "Earth Day Anthem" was penned with the lyrics set to the tune of Beethoven's "Ode to Joy." Sing it if you dare (and do not sing it too loudly because we would never want to contribute to noise pollution):

> Joyful, joyful we adore our
>
> Earth in all its wonderment
>
> Simple gifts of nature that all join into a paradise.
>
> Now we must resolve to protect her
>
> Show her our love throughout all time
>
> With our gentle hand and touch
>
> We make our home a newborn world.
>
> Now we must resolve to protect her
>
> Show her our love throughout all time
>
> With our gentle hand and touch
>
> We make our home a newborn world.

Aren't you so happy that the lyrics are public domain? What is my point? Answer: these greenies are sold out with their hearts, souls, minds, and strength. Forward, march. Yes sir. No ma'am. If only more church members were as committed!

Although it is a problematic truth, "brainwashing" has been replaced with "greenwashing." Greenwashing is used by organizations in an attempt to promote themselves as green so that they will gain revenue or support. Corporations and companies "greenwash" when they spend more money on looking green than they spend on actually being green. In other words, these companies fritter away money in an attempt to portray themselves as green-friendly rather than literally taking care of the environment. That is the heart of greenwashing. I prefer the idea of "astroturfing" better, but then, via the Internet, I found out that "astroturfing" is an actual word used to describe public relations campaigns by which companies hide their real message through independent third parties.

Christians could learn tenacity, unity, purpose, and perseverance from many environmentalists. Robust people carrying a robust message usually result in converts. Setting their sights high, Earth Day 2012 had for its motto "Mobilize the Earth." I like "Make Disciples" better.

Inconvenient Truths

Playing off of the popular Al Gore documentary, let's look at five truths, stemming either directly or indirectly from the Bible, that can be very inconvenient to green activists or Christians who straddle the eco-fence of excessive environmentalism. These truths are designed to help you navigate through the treacherous waters of the Greenpeace theology.

Inconvenient Truth #1: Greening/environmentalism blurs the line between the Creator and the creation.

God created men and women to be men and women who worship. People must worship. God has set "eternity in their hearts" (Ecclesiastes 3:11). Built into every person's warp and woof is the principle of worship. If they do not worship God, then their desire to worship will shift to worshiping something or someone in God's universe. Sadly, countless people even worship the creation.

> Therefore God gave them up in the lusts of their hearts to impurity, to the dishonoring of their bodies among themselves, because they exchanged the truth about God for a lie and worshiped and served the creature rather than the Creator, who is blessed forever! Amen. (Romans 1:24–25)

Sin torques humans so much that they will adulate created things instead of their Creator. The essence of idolatry is the veneration of something made or someone besides the Lord.

Idolatry illustrates its insidious nature by taking something good and then worshiping it. The creation is not bad, but it is bad to worship it. Sex is not bad, but it must not be worshiped. Food. Sports. Family.

Paul sternly warned the Corinthians:

> Do not be idolaters as some of them were; as it is written, "The people sat down to eat and drink and rose up to play." (1 Corinthians 10:7)

Paul, quoting Exodus 32, brings up the Israelites who were caught up in idol worship and were subsequently killed by God Himself. Moses further described the incident:

> And as soon as he came near the camp and saw the calf and the dancing, Moses' anger burned hot, and he threw the tablets out of his hands and broke them at the foot of the mountain. He took the calf that they had made and burned it with fire and ground it to powder and scattered it on the water and made the people of Israel drink it. (Exodus 32:19–20)

What if our president stood in front of Congress and took an acetylene torch to the Declaration of Independence? The shock that you would feel as you watched it on CNN gives you an idea of what Israel must have felt when Moses literally broke the Ten Commandments before their very eyes. Actually, the Israelites did more than feel. Moses forced the sinful idolaters to drink the effects of their sin, ensuring that the vile sin would not be repeated unless the Israelites would demonstrate their grossness by searching for gold in their own waste. Yuck is an understatement. Idolatry is grosser than any excrement scavenger hunt.

Most readers realize that worshiping a literal stone or carved piece of wood is wrong, but they often forget the siren-song nuances of modern day idolatry. For example, when people give undue attention to something then *that* is idolatry. What is a little undue attention when it comes to my children? When humans regard something in place of God, that is idolatry. Why can't I value my marriage supremely? Giving undue regard to someone is idolatry. Valuing something too highly is idolatry. J.C. Ryle defined idolatry as "worship, in which the honor due to the Triune God, and to God only, is given to some of His creatures, or to some invention of His creatures."[1]

---

[1] J.C. Ryle, *Idolatry*, accessed from http://www.biblebb.com/files/ryle/warn8.htm.

Avoid taking something good and making it into the be-all and end-all of your life. Scripture regularly implores people to avoid a "divided heart," a heart not fully devoted to the worship of God. Allegiance to the environment and to God is divided and, therefore, misdirected. God alone must receive worship. The formula, "God plus," must be thrown away like an old fashioned soda can. Strike that. It must be taken to the recycle bin. Too often, "green" Christians have hearts less than fully directed toward God. Beware.

Inconvenient Truth #2: Greening forgets the creation mandate.

The creation mandate is taken from Genesis 1:28:

> And God blessed them. And God said to them, "Be fruitful and multiply and fill the earth and subdue it, and have dominion over the fish of the sea and over the birds of the heavens and over every living thing that moves on the earth."

God blesses His human creatures and commands them to reproduce to the extent that their children will bring the world into subjection. Humanity, acting on behalf of God, must rule over everything. God wanted Adam and his posterity to act as God's representatives on earth. Be fruitful. Multiply. Fill the earth. Subdue it. Have dominion over fish, birds, and every living thing. God commanded man to be the steward of God's handiwork. Mankind was given preeminence over every created thing. Man's mandate, as an image bearer, is not to be taken lightly, even if it is not politically correct.

A.M. Wolters captures the drama of God creating man and then giving them a foundational command:

> There is something highly dramatic about the moment when God has created a creature to be like Himself and then clears his throat, so to speak, to address him. This is the moment when man, the crown of creation, is to be told what God's plan is for him, why God has placed him in this world, what his marching orders are for the long campaign ahead. It is the significant moment when God almighty enters into communication with flesh-and-blood man, initiates the revelation-and-response structure of man's total life, making it into religion. It is at this mo-

ment of cosmic significance that God gives the command: "Fill the earth and subdue it!"[2]

Man, as God's regent, was not called to rape and pillage the world with a bulldozer-everything clear-cut mentality. Intentional pollution due to laziness, profit, or carelessness is never righteous. But it is unrighteous to ignore Genesis 1:28 or to allow God's creation mandate to take a back seat to the preservation of the world and all it contains. Greening and its philosophy is not mentioned in Genesis or in any other biblical book, therefore, it must be subordinated to the creation mandate. Man must execute his faithful stewardship over God's creation by ruling and governing what God made for man.

Inconvenient Truth #3: There is something worse than oil spills.

As bad as the Exxon Valdez oil spill was, it officially ranks as only the thirty-sixth worse oil spill of all time. Eleven million gallons of crude flooding into the Prince William Sound was horrific, but in 1991 the Iraqi military purposely dumped 380–520 million gallons of crude into the Persian Gulf in an attempt to halt the American soldiers from landing. Everyone agrees that oil spills should be avoided and cleanup efforts supported. Visuals of oil-saturated pelicans and other wildlife are hard to digest. But there is a greater tragedy that occurs much more frequently than oil spills. Sadly, this tragedy cannot be tangibly measured with units like gallons. Many unwitting Christians fervently participate in environmental campaigns and agendas driven by pagan and worldly thinking. Helping at a beach cleanup is not my concern, rather my distress is myopic thinking that views planet earth as the focal point.

In Isaiah 6:3, the prophet Isaiah saw a vision of the angels hovering around the throne of God. Isaiah heard the angels say to each other, in a type of antiphonal refrain, "Holy, holy, holy is the LORD of hosts; the whole earth is full of his glory!" The angels proclaim that the earth is like a launching pad for the glory of God to be displayed. The earth must serve as a means for God to be worshiped and never as the object of worship. Creation should reflect and magnify God and God alone. Isaiah later quotes God declaring, "I am the LORD; that is my name; my glory I give to no other" (Isaiah 42:8). The earth's wonders should act as a catalyst in glorifying God. The planet must not be worshiped. It is one thing to acknowledge "earth idolatry," but it is quite another to avoid it.

[2]A.M. Wolters, *Scientific Contributions of the PU for CHE, IRS*, study pamphlet no. 382 (October 1999), 33.

God is concerned with His own glory, namely the redemptive work of Jesus Christ the Savior. To put it bluntly, one elect soul is worth more to God than twenty million planets. The church exists to exalt the saving work of the Son of God. The church does not exist to pander to the mandates of Greenpeace. What if we saved the planet but every person on it went to perdition? Additionally, when the church joins unbelieving eco-friendlies arm in arm to crusade against carbon emissions, the unbeliever's main problem of sin and alienation from God gets ignored because the perceived enemy of carbon emissions is the focus of the battle.

In our society dominated by the "tyranny of the urgent," needs and wants all clamor to be heard as imperative. The church must embrace Paul's hierarchical importance structure:

> For I delivered to you as of *first importance* what I also received: that Christ died for our sins in accordance with the Scriptures, that he was buried, that he was raised on the third day in accordance with the Scriptures. (1 Corinthians 15:3–4, emphasis added)

Inconvenient Truth #4: The world will not outlive its usefulness.

Californians for Population Stabilization (CAPS) is pushing for the leaders of Earth Day to focus upon the terrors of human overpopulation. For CAPS, overpopulation is as dreaded as the use of plastic grocery bags. Filling the earth is mandated by God, and it does not seem like God is too concerned about overpopulation in light of Genesis 1:28:

> And God blessed them. And God said to them, "Be fruitful and multiply and fill the earth and subdue it, and have dominion over the fish of the sea and over the birds of the heavens and over every living thing that moves on the earth."

Don't fall for the perennial rumpus about overpopulation. God must be obeyed and trusted. Let the results fall into God's lap to provide for them (See Matthew 6). Jesus is building His church and when the last elect person believes, then it will be the beginning of the end of the current configuration of the world. God is sovereign and eternal. The earth is neither sovereign nor eternal. Paul teaches that truth:

> For the creation waits with eager longing for the revealing of the sons of God. For the creation was subjected to futil-

ity, not willingly, but because of him who subjected it, in hope that the creation itself will be set free from its bondage to corruption and obtain the freedom of the glory of the children of God. (Romans 8:19–21)

The world has a built-in shelf life. Based upon its current configuration, the earth was not meant to last forever.

Inconvenient Truth #5: There are two prominent earth days in the Bible.

God has two earth days in the Bible—one was in the past and one will be in the future. The emphasis is on the whole "earth" more than on "days." To be technical, neither of the following is a literal twenty-four-hour day, but the point should not be missed—the earth was and will be completely destroyed. Therefore, do not worship what is ephemeral and disposable.

God flooded the whole earth in the days of Noah. The Bible clearly states,

> The flood continued forty days on the earth. The waters increased and bore up the ark, and it rose high above the earth. The waters prevailed and increased greatly on the earth, and the ark floated on the face of the waters. And the waters prevailed so mightily on the earth that all the high mountains under the whole heaven were covered. The waters prevailed above the mountains, covering them fifteen cubits deep. And all flesh died that moved on the earth, birds, livestock, beasts, all swarming creatures that swarm on the earth, and all mankind. Everything on the dry land in whose nostrils was the breath of life died. He blotted out every living thing that was on the face of the ground, man and animals and creeping things and birds of the heavens. They were blotted out from the earth. Only Noah was left, and those who were with him in the ark. And the waters prevailed on the earth 150 days. (Genesis 7:17–24)

The death toll caused by God's flood upon unrepentant people is simply staggering. Too often, the story of Noah's ark is reduced to an infant's crib mobile with animals harmlessly spinning around while junior goos and gaas with baby talk. God exacted righteous judgment on everyone except eight people, and that includes the drowning of every infant on the face of the earth. There was mass and wholesale adjudication upon every person who was outside of the ark. God did not spare plants, animals, or the environment. The environment was completely flooded. Global flooding.

There is another flood coming in the future. It will be the second major earth day. It will not be a flood of water because God promised He would not do that, but it will be a global flood of fire. Peter writes,

> But the day of the Lord will come like a thief, and then the heavens will pass away with a roar, and the heavenly bodies will be burned up and dissolved, and the earth and the works that are done on it will be exposed. Since all these things are thus to be dissolved, what sort of people ought you to be in lives of holiness and godliness, waiting for and hastening the coming of the day of God, because of which the heavens will be set on fire and dissolved, and the heavenly bodies will melt as they burn! But according to his promise we are waiting for new heavens and a new earth in which righteousness dwells. (2 Peter 3:10–13)

At the end of time, God will need to cleanse the earth and He will do it with a purifying fire. Therefore, why devote your entire life to "serving" the planet earth that is doomed to be dissolved? Serve the Lord Jesus and strive for eternal things. Serve something that will last.

However, Christians should never pollute, ruin or waste God's creation just because they know that God will eventually purify the earth with fire. It is only God's prerogative to burn the earth. Christians should be respectful of anything that is owned by God and that includes the earth. But do not pollute your minds with confusing the permanent with the temporary!

Conclusion

When a church or an individual church member begins to adorn the livery of green theology, something will suffer. Greening takes away time, money, and focus from the Great Commission and from the Lord Jesus Christ Himself. Greenpeace protestors regularly handcuff themselves to fishing boats in the ocean in an attempt to halt fishing. Christians, do not shackle yourselves to the boat of overemphasizing the greening of the church or eco-friendliness in general.

Response

1. Would you buy a hemp-bound Bible? Would you buy a fair trade, Message translation?

2. Would you be willing to cause a fight at the annual business meeting over water-free urinals?

3. How much patience will you extend to new Christians who are very eco-friendly?

4. Do you give as much energy to the gospel and its promotion as you give to recycling?

5. Green-speak, the vocabulary of the eco-movement, grows by the solar day. Are you better versed in the first list full of environmental verbiage or the second?

Green-speak:

- Toxicity
- Eco-broker
- FSC-certified wood
- Geothermal
- Native landscaping
- Runoff
- Carbon offsetting
- Fair trade
- Solar PV
- Low-impact living
- Renewable resources
- Sustainable agriculture
- Post-consumer recycled
- Vermicomposting

Gospel-speak:

- Propitiation
- Vicarious atonement
- Redemption
- Triune
- Substitution
- Reconciliation
- Expiation
- Forgiveness
- Justification
- Sanctification

Green speech needs to be replaced with "gospel speech!"

Chapter Nine

. . .

White Lie #9: God Fits in a Box

. . .

Early one morning in North Hollywood, I shushed the neighbor's cat, hoping to motivate it to get out from under my car. Double shush. Still nothing. As I moved closer, the reason for its stillness dawned on me. It was dead. The cat had a name. It was Jumps-a-lot. True! But sadly, Jumps-a-lot was now Dead-a-lot. Since it was 4:30 in the morning, I knew the owner would not appreciate a rap on the door, so I put the lifeless cat's body into a garbage liner and slid it under the bushes. I would return in the afternoon and then break the bad news. Oh, I forgot to tell you that I placed the garbage liner inside of a cardboard box.

Did I also forget to tell you that it would be a hot summer day in California? When I put Jumps-a-lot into the trash liner and box, his body was still warm and flaccid. After several hours, rigor mortis set in and the feline's body conformed stiffly to the exact contours of the box. The depletion of adenosine triphosphate in the cat's muscle tissues made box extraction a cadaveric *cat*-astrophe (pun intended).

Conformed to a box. Jumps-a-lot in a box. God in a box. How often do we hear people bellow, "do not put God in a box?" Often. What do they mean? It is a figure of speech designed to keep God from humanistic constructs that are not biblical. In other words, God is so big and grand that He cannot be contained.

I forgot to mention another thing. The garbage liner ripped open when I was trying to bury the cat. Whew. The smell. The smell of death.

It took days for that smell to get out of my nostrils and my mind. What is grosser than the smell of the decaying body of a cat? Odor. Oh dear. Any whiff of presenting a manageable, small God. A "God in a box." Many modern evangelicals have been jettisoning the transcendent greatness of God by only teaching His immanence (closeness). God is close (think incarnation and Immanuel), but He is simultaneously transcendent (other, different and above).

Grasping God

The modern-day white lie teaches that God *can* be fully grasped. The lie is that God can be tamed or domesticated. While God can be understood through His Word, God, Himself is incomprehensible. God is great. God is truly awesome. When David wrote "Great is the LORD, and greatly to be praised, and his greatness is unsearchable" (Psalm 145:3), was it rhetoric? Hyperbole? J.I. Packer said, "Theology states this by describing him as incomprehensible—not in the sense that logic is somehow different for him from what it is for us, so that we cannot follow the workings of his mind at all, but in the sense that we can never understand him fully, just because he is infinite and we are finite."[1]

Who alone can fully and wholly understand all there is to know about God and His works? God's incomprehensibility severely limits the answer to this question. Only the Triune God can comprehend Himself. We, as finite humans, can barely understand ourselves, let alone the transcendent and eternal God. Whether before the Fall of Adam, after the Fall, or in glory, God is too awesome for created beings to fully wrap their minds around.

People are starving for the glory and greatness of God, and this perfection satisfies the longing soul that senses the hunger pangs of knowing God. It truly shows God's immensity next to the tiny nature of mankind.

God reveals to us in the Bible that He is far beyond human reasoning and higher than any of man's logical systems of thought or philosophy. God is infinite and we do not have the capacity to understand or explain God exhaustively. Robert Morey says that God is not mentally "manageable!"[2] He will not fit into our preconceived molds of who we think God should be and how He should conduct Himself. Morey goes on to say:

[1]J.I. Packer, *Concise Theology* (Wheaton, IL: Tyndale House Publishers, Inc., 1993), 51.
[2]Robert A. Morey, *Battle of the Gods* (Southbridge, MA: Crown, 1989), 161.

He will always be *beyond* our grasp. He is too high for us to scale and too deep for us to fathom. We cannot get God in a box. The finite span of the human mind will never encompass the infinite God of Scripture.[3]

This is simply the "God-ness" of God. A.W. Tozer described this attribute saying, "To say that God is infinite is to say that He is measureless. Measurement is the way created things have of accounting for themselves. It describes limitations, imperfections, and cannot apply to God."[4] Weight, length, space, and other units of measure cannot apply to God. He is above, beyond, and outside of calculation and computation. Slide rules, calculators, and the fastest computers cannot assess, quantify, or appraise the "great and awesome God" (Deuteronomy 7:21).

The book of Job expresses the praiseworthiness of God's incomprehensibility. Job 26:14 says, "Behold, these are but the outskirts of his ways, and how small a whisper do we hear of him! But the thunder of his power who can understand?" God is so wonderful that even the edges of His ways, the mere and momentary glimpses of His rule, still promote praise and repentance. If the meager fringe of God is this great, how incredible must be the inner workings of God?

We see man's limitation often in the corpus of the Old Testament, especially in Ezekiel as the prophet is reduced to employing similes such as "like," and "as the appearance" as he tries to mentally grasp and then put into words the manifestation of God:

> And upward from what had the appearance of his waist I saw as it were gleaming metal, like the appearance of fire enclosed all around. And downward from what had the appearance of his waist I saw as it were the appearance of fire, and there was brightness around him. Like the appearance of the bow that is in the cloud on the day of rain, so was the appearance of the brightness all around. Such was the appearance of the likeness of the glory of the LORD. And when I saw it, I fell on my face, and I heard the voice of one speaking. (Ezekiel 1:27–28)

---

[3]Ibid., 161.
[4]A.W. Tozer, *The Knowledge of the Holy* (Raleigh, NC: Lulu Press, Inc, 2013), Ebook.

God's Great Works

Not only is God Himself incomprehensible, but so too are His works.[5] Two favorite verses of many who ponder the gravity of God are:

> For my thoughts are not your thoughts, neither are your ways my ways, declares the LORD. For as the heavens are higher than the earth, so are my ways higher than your ways and my thoughts than your thoughts. (Isaiah 55:8–9)

Have you ever asked yourself the context of these verses? Even the immediate context is shown by the first word in verse 8 with the word, "For." This word links these verses with what was just said. In what context or manner is the LORD different in His thinking? Far from being a general statement of His incomprehensibility,[6] these verses show that God does not think and act in a way that even remotely resembles created human beings. Do you see the connection?

> "Seek the LORD while he may be found; call upon him while he is near; let the wicked forsake his way, and the unrighteous man his thoughts; let him return to the LORD, that he may have compassion on him, and to our God, for he will abundantly pardon." (Isaiah 55:6–7)

If you were God, consider what you might do to a rebellious, stiff-necked, and sinful people. How would you react to willful insubordination and overt transgression committed against you? Isaiah 55:7 states that the God of the Bible copiously pardons and forgives![7] But thanks be

---

[5]This only makes sense since you cannot separate who a person is from what he or she does. How much more must this apply to the Godhead!

[6]"Verses 8–9 do not refer simply to the inscrutable character of God's ways and thoughts; for, in the light of v. 7, it is clear that there is a stress on the moral difference. God's thoughts and ways are in fact governed by righteousness—his righteousness—and his effective word therefore accomplishes a moral purpose, the reclamation of the sinner from the error and wickedness of his ways." Frank E. Gabelein, Gen. Ed., *The Expositor's Bible Commentary* (Grand Rapids, MI: The Zondervan Corporation, 1986), 6:313.

[7]The Hebrew root word for "abundantly" in Isa 55:7 is "hbr" and the lexical meaning contains the idea of "great," "many," or "frequent." HALOT Lexicon states the construction in Isa 55:7, with the infinitive, yields the meaning, "to make something manifold, plentiful, continuous." L. Koehler, W. Baumgartner, and J.J. Stamm, *The Hebrew and Aramaic Lexicon of the Old Testament*, Trans., ed., M.E.J. Richardson (Leiden: Brill, 1994–2000), BibleWorks, v7.0.

to God, our thoughts are nothing like His gracious and merciful thoughts of compassion for His beloved ones.

Similarly, this is why the apostle Paul can barely contain himself at the end of Romans 11. He is effervescent with praise proclaiming,

> Oh, the depth of the riches and wisdom and knowledge of God! How unsearchable are his judgments and how inscrutable his ways!
>
> > "For who has known the mind of the Lord,
> >
> > or who has been his counselor?"
> >
> > "Or who has given a gift to him
> >
> > that he might be repaid?"
>
> For from him and through him and to him are all things. To him be glory forever. Amen. (Romans 11:33–36)

Chapter 11 ends with this paean of praise to the incomprehensible wisdom and utter mercy of our God. This praise was for God's plan in salvation of both Israel and the Gentiles, but there are more reasons for Paul to worship His Lord. John MacArthur says, "This doxology is a fitting response not only to God's future plans for Israel (chaps. 9–11), but to Paul's entire discussion of justification by faith (chaps. 1–11)."[8] God is seen as marvelous when He sovereignly deals with His creatures, both Israel and the Gentiles.

Digging deeper, "the depth" of God's wisdom and knowledge reveals, in the original language, an extreme reaching into the depths or going so deep that we are over our heads.[9] It is too extreme to be comprehended. God's wisdom is inexhaustible. Southern Baptist scholar A.T. Robertson appropriately relates this verse to the incomprehensibility of God saying,

---

[8]John F. MacArthur, Jr., *The MacArthur Study Bible* (Nashville, TN: Word Bibles, 1997), 1716.

[9]BDAG Lexicon states that "depth" (*bathos*) is metaphorically used to show "inexhaustible abundance, immense amount." Romans 8:39 similarly uses this word, "nor height, nor depth, nor any other created thing, will be able to separate us from the love of God, which is in Christ Jesus our Lord." Walter Bauer, Frederick W. Danker, William F. Arndt, and F. Wilbur Gingrich, *A Greek-English Lexicon of the New Testament and Other Early Christian Literature*, 3rd ed. (Chicago, IL: University of Chicago Press, 2000), BibleWorks. v.9.

"Paul's argument concerning God's elective grace and goodness has carried him to the heights and now he pauses on the edge of the precipice as he contemplates God's wisdom and knowledge, fully conscious of his inability to sound the bottom with the plummet of human reason and words."[10] Paul's lack of full understanding did not impede his ability to worship and glorify the God of His salvation.

God's wisdom is too deep, but so are His "judgments" and His "ways" (also in Romans 11:33). "Unfathomable" is a rare word in the Bible, and it is used to designate something that is beyond tracing out. God's footprints cannot be tracked or traced. In verse 34, Paul quotes Isaiah 40:13, and demonstrates that God had no help in designing this gracious plan. In verse 35, Job 41:11 is freely quoted and demonstrates that God is the only responsible party for all His deeds. God could never be compared to the fox that is hunted by the hounds of men. God is the sovereign and exalted One who must receive glory.

Jumps-a-lot has probably decomposed by now. Even his skeleton has probably turned to dust. Let's leave a manageable God six feet under as well. R.I.P.

Responding to an Awesome God

God's incomprehensibility prods you to:

1. Wonder and Praise.

Does this "unmanageable" God repel you or attract you? The biblical and worshipful response is awe, wonder, and praise. Oh, worship the King that said,

> Thus says the LORD, the King of Israel
>
> and his Redeemer, the LORD of hosts:
>
> "I am the first and I am the last;
>
> besides me there is no god.
>
> Who is like me? Let him proclaim it.
>
> Let him declare and set it before me,
>
> since I appointed an ancient people.
>
> Let them declare what is to come, and what will happen." (Isaiah 44:6–7)

---

[10]A.T. Roberson, *Word Pictures in the New Testament* (Grand Rapids, MI: Baker Book House, 1931) BibleWorks. v7.0.

Are you rejoicing that over two thousand years ago this great God cloaked Himself with humanity to die in the place of sinners like you? Salvation through Jesus Christ is no longer incomprehensible. Angels had to stoop to examine such a doctrine and reality, but the Second Person of the Trinity, full of grace and truth, pitched His tabernacle among us in order to rescue us from the deserved wrath of God.

2. Repentance.

After God turned the questioning tables on Job, he could only respond to God's incomprehensibility by relinquishing any ideas of being God and then repenting.

> Then Job answered the LORD and said:
>
> "I know that you can do all things,
>
> and that no purpose of yours can be thwarted.
>
> 'Who is this that hides counsel without knowedge?'
>
> Therefore I have uttered what I did not understand,
>
> things too wonderful for me, which I did not know.
>
> 'Hear, and I will speak;
>
> I will question you, and you make it known to me.'
>
> I had heard of you by the hearing of the ear,
>
> but now my eye sees you;
>
> therefore, I despise myself,
>
> and repent in dust and ashes." (Job 42:1–6)

Systematic theologian Robert Culver elucidated on the response to God's incomprehensibility by saying, "These things do not inspire long speeches, rather stumbling works of repentance and silence, as illustrated by Job's excellent example (Job 38–40)."[11] If you have been like Job, questioning God due to a major and real trial in your life, the right response is repentance and acquiescence to God and His perfect plans (even if they cannot be understood by you now).

3. Obey what you know (do not become paralyzed with things that God does not want you to know).

---

[11]Robert Duncan Culver, *Systematic Theology* (Geanies House, Fearn, Ross-shire, Great Britain: Mentor, 2005), 91.

A perennial favorite verse with all Bible students is Deuteronomy 29:29. Strike that! A perennial and *partial* favorite is Deuteronomy 29:29. Can you quote the whole verse? Moses said to Israel, "The secret things belong to the LORD our God." Is there more to the quote? The full quote is:

> The secret things belong to the LORD our God, but the things that are revealed belong to us and to our children forever, that we may do all the words of this law. (Deuteronomy 29:29)

Did you see that? There are many areas of life that we could never comprehend, but this knowledge, or lack thereof, should not incapacitate us from obeying what we do know as clear and understandable. Solomon gives similar wise advice saying,

> As you do not know the way the spirit comes to the bones in the womb of a woman with child, so you do not know the work of God who makes everything. In the morning sow your seed, and at evening withhold not your hand, for you do not know which will prosper, this or that, or whether both alike will be good. (Ecclesiastes 11:5–6)

Old Testament scholar J.S. Wright affirms this as he echoes the sentiment of Solomon saying,

> Few parents understand precisely how a baby is formed, but most follow the rules of common sense for the welfare of the mother and the unborn child. This is exactly the application that the Teacher makes here to the plan of God. Indeed, it illustrates the whole theme of the book. We cannot understand all the ways God works to fulfill his plan, but we can follow God's rules for daily living and thus help bring God's purpose to birth.[12]

It is not mandatory to understand the inner workings of the Godhead to obey Him. Just as human parents expect their children to obey even if the children do not grasp rationally all there is to the reasons for the commands, so God desires obedience. Solomon goes on to say,

---

[12]J. Stafford Wright, "Ecclesiastes," in "Psalms, Proverbs, Ecclesiastes, Song of Solomon," vol. 5 of *The Expositor's Bible Commentary* (Grand Rapids, MI: Zondervan, 1990), 1189.

> The end of the matter; all has been heard. Fear God and keep his commandments, for this is the whole duty of man. For God will bring every deed into judgment, with every secret thing, whether good or evil. (Ecclesiastes 12:13–14)

Daniel Webster has supposedly said, "My greatest thought is my accountability to God." Our greatest thoughts should not be on the mind of God that He has chosen not to reveal. The story goes that William Phelps taught English literature at Yale for forty-one years until his retirement in 1933. Correcting an exam just before Christmas one year, Phelps stumbled on this note: "God only knows the answer to this question. Merry Christmas." Phelps returned the paper with this note: "God gets an A. You get an F. Happy New Year." Focus on the revealed will of God, especially in the New Testament epistles.

4. Do not go to the other extreme and assume that God cannot be known at all.

We are still required to know as much about God as is revealed in Holy Writ. Jeremiah knew much about God, and so can you (you just cannot go beyond what God has set forth in His Word):

> Thus says the LORD: "Let not the wise man boast in his wisdom, let not the mighty man boast in his might, let not the rich man boast in his riches, but let him who boasts boast in this, that he understands and knows me, that I am the LORD who practices steadfast love, justice, and righteousness in the earth. For in these things I delight, declares the LORD." (Jeremiah 9:23–24)

5. Live by faith!

Job ultimately accepted the fact that he was not able to understand the infinite God. Instead, he resorted to living by faith. Join the long line of others who have rejected the option of walking by sight and walk by faith:

> Behold, his soul is puffed up; it is not upright within him, but the righteous shall live by his faith. (Habakkuk 2:4)

> I have been crucified with Christ. It is no longer I who live, but Christ who lives in me. And the life I now live in the flesh I live by faith in the Son of God, who loved me and gave himself for me. (Galatians 2:20)

Now it is evident that no one is justified before God by the law, for "The righteous shall live by faith." (Galatians 3:11)

but my righteous one shall live by faith, and if he shrinks back, my soul has no pleasure in him. (Hebrews 10:38)

Forget trying to find the solution to every theological, personal, and social problem. Instead, acknowledge with Job that God is the one "who does great and unsearchable things, wonders without number" (Job 5:9). Rest. Submit. Walk by faith.

6. Put a dagger in pride.

Contrary to popular philosophy, man is not the measure of all things. Join Charles Spurgeon and say,

> Other subjects we can comprehend and grapple with; in them we feel a kind of self-content, and go on our way with the thought, "Behold I am wise." But when we come to this master science, finding that our plumb line cannot sound its depth, and that our eagle eye cannot see its height, we turn away with the thought "I am but of yesterday and know nothing."[13]

Homework

1. Read Job 38–42. Is there any trial in your life that should cause you to question the goodness of God? Suppress those feelings and remember the nature of God. Hint: Remember Job 1 and all the trials Job endured. Did Job experience more than you are going through right now? What or who sustained Job? Is Job's God your God?

2. Do not forget to read the entire Bible, especially the Old Testament. This discipline will help you see the transcendent nature of God. It will reap a good balance to the "user-friendly" God that is so often promoted in modern day evangelicalism. Only a spiritual Pinocchio would fall for the white lie that understands and presents God as mentally manageable. "Tame" and "God" are not compatible as modifier and noun. No one has God "by the tail," as if God were domesticated.

---

[13] A Sermon (No. 1) Delivered on Sabbath Morning, January 7, 1855, by the Rev. C.H. Spurgeon at New Park Street Chapel, Southwark, accessed from http://www.spurgeon.org/sermons/0001.php.

3. Don't get caught up in trying to use the Bible to solve every problem you encounter. The Bible was not meant to be an exhaustive answer book to difficulties. Read the Word to wash your mind from thinking in a man-centered manner. "Trust the LORD with all your heart" (Proverbs 3:5a).

4. Reflect upon the opposite truth: God, the incomprehensible One, does fully comprehend His people. God knows believers completely, yet still loves them. Now that is humanly incomprehensible! And wonderful. Luther would agree:

> Mere human reason can never comprehend how God is good and merciful; and therefore you make to yourself a god of your own fancy, who hardens nobody, condemns nobody, pities everybody. You cannot comprehend how a just God can condemn those who are born into sin, and cannot help themselves, but must, by a necessity of their natural constitution, continue in, and remain children of wrath. The answer is, God is incomprehensible throughout, and therefore His justice, as well as His other attributes, must be incomprehensible. It is only on this very ground that St. Paul exclaims, "O the depth of the riches of the knowledge of God! How unsearchable are His judgments, and His ways past finding out!"[14]

5. Read, or sing, this song of praise:

"The LORD, How Wondrous Are His Ways"

The Lord, how wondrous are His ways!

How firm His truth! how large His grace!

He takes His mercy for His throne,

And thence He makes His glories known.

Not half so high His power hath spread

The starry heav'ns above our head,

As His rich love exceeds our praise,

---

[14]Quoted in Robert Haldane, *Exposition of the Epistle to the Romans* (MacDill, FL: MacDonald Publishing Company, 1839), 492.

Exceeds the highest hopes we raise.

Not half so far hath nature placed

The rising morning from the west,

As His forgiving grace removes

The daily guilt of those He loves.

How slowly doth His wrath arise!

On swifter wings salvation flies;

And if He lets His anger burn,

How soon His frowns to pity turn.

Amidst His wrath compassion shines;

His strokes are lighter than our sins;

And while His rod corrects His saints,

His ear indulges their complaints.

So fathers their young sons chastise

With gentle hand and melting eyes;

The children weep beneath the smart,

And move the pity of their heart.

The mighty God, the wise and just,

Knows that our frame is feeble dust;

And will no heavy loads impose

Beyond the strength that He bestows.

He knows how soon our nature dies,

Blasted by every wind that flies;

Like grass we spring, and die as soon,

Or morning flowers that fade at noon.

But His eternal love is sure

To all the saints, and shall endure;

From age to age His truth shall reign,

Nor children's children hope in vain.

Isaac Watts, *The Psalms of David*, 1719.[15]

---

[15]Accessed from http://www.cyberhymnal.org/htm/l/h/lhowwond.htm.

Chapter Ten

. . .

White Lie #10: The Weather Is a Thing

. . .

A.W. Pink's *The Sovereignty of God* rocked my world.[1] I read it when I was a new Christian and pretty much everything changed. Okay, my mind changed. I repented of my low view of God. God was sovereign in name and by His actions. Lord meant "Lord" and not quasi-Lord or almost-Lord. Pink's third chapter entitled "Sovereignty of God in Administration" particularly piqued my interest. It devastated my thinking. The truth elaborated there grabbed my attention and demanded me to think differently. Pink's words still reverberate in my psyche. Why? First, he discusses scriptural concepts, and the Bible has a wonderful way of burrowing into your soul. Second, I got so convicted about my complaining about every bit of weather that did not please me! Pink's words sound like they originated from my high school football coach. Pink "yells:"

> What a declaration is this: "He sendeth forth His commandment upon earth: His word runneth very swiftly. *He giveth* snow like wool: *He scattereth* the hoar frost like ashes. *He casteth forth* His ice like morsels: who can stand before *His cold? He sendeth* out His word, and melteth them: *He causeth His wind to blow*, and the waters flow" (Psa. 147:15–18). The mutations of the elements are beneath

---

[1] I understand some of Pink's hyper-Calvinistic tendencies; I still really appreciate this book and *The Attributes of God*. Both are highly recommended. For what it is worth, I am usually a little wary of people who run around quoting A.W. Pink. There are exceptions!

God's Sovereign control. It is *God* who withholds the rain, and it is *God* who gives the rain when He wills, where He wills, as He wills, and on whom He wills. Weather Bureaus may attempt to give forecasts of the weather, but how frequently God mocks their calculations! Sun 'spots,' the varying activities of the planets, the appearing and disappearing of comets (to which abnormal weather is sometimes attributed), atmospheric disturbances, are merely secondary causes, for behind them all is God Himself. Let His Word speak once more: "And also *I have withholden the rain* from you, when there were yet three months to the harvest: *and I caused* it to rain upon one city, and caused it not to rain upon another city: one piece was rained upon, and the piece whereon it rain not withered. So two or three cities wandered unto one city, to drink water; but they were not satisfied: yet have ye not returned unto Me, saith the LORD. *I have smitten you with blasting and mildew*: when your gardens and your vineyards and your fig trees and your olive trees increased, the palmerworm devoured them: yet have ye not returned unto Me, saith the LORD. *I have sent among you the pestilence* after the manner of Egypt: your young men have I slain with the sword, and have taken away your horses; and I have made the stink of your camps to come up into your nostrils: yet have ye not returned unto Me, saith the LORD" (Amos 4:7–10).

Truly, then, God governs inanimate matter. Earth and air, fire and water, hail and snow, stormy winds and angry seas, all perform the word of His power and fulfill His Sovereign pleasure. Therefore, when we complain about the weather we are, in reality, murmuring against God.[2]

My guess is that you now want to buy the book. Good news: the book is free online. Google it! My grandparents needed to read Pink's chapter on the weather and the sovereignty of God. They worried about the weather even on a sunny day. One never knows? Armed with their Realistic WeatherRadio Deskube from 1970, they listened intently for the next round of hail, tornados, or hurricane. If it was not worrying, it

---

[2]Both quotes are accessed from http://www.reformed.org/books/pink/.

was complaining. Too hot. Too cold. Too "just right." At least we can be more sophisticated with our worry courtesy of The Weather Channel.

If you had to choose something to comfort and guide you, would you grab hold of the doctrine of the sovereignty of God or would you reach for the faux-walnut paneling weather radio cube, fit for the side of my mother's old station wagon? The weather cube was made in Taiwan and sold for $17.95. If this illustration is beyond your grasp, or age, just think about the weather app you have on your smartphone. How often do you check it? While there is nothing inherently wrong with knowing the weather, there is always something wrong with complaining about God's weather. Weather that He chose.

Professional Complainers

Some temptations occur irregularly. The temptations that rear their ugly head regularly are even more dangerous. Beware of daily temptations like the weather. Well, the weather is not the temptation, but because of the weather and how often it changes, it yields a perfect opportunity for people to complain and murmur. Doesn't the weather affect you every single day of the year? It influences peoples' clothing choices, travel plans, and even their moods and attitudes. Complaining about the weather is practically a sport practically everybody competes in today. Professional, not collegiate.

Years ago, the UPI news service predicted that El Niño would be responsible for continued wet weather in the West and South, along with warmer and drier conditions in the Midwest and New England. "El Niño most strongly impacts U.S. weather patterns during the winter by shifting the jet stream and storm track toward the southern tier of the country," said Jim Laver, director of NOAA's Climate Research Center. "As a result, increased storminess is expected across the southern United States." El Niño seems to be making a comeback, but not without some problems for retired naval pilot, Al Nino (you simply cannot make this up). Al has received more than 100 telephones calls "from people blaming him for El Niño storms." This ludicrous example illustrates what many Christians do under a sophisticated cloak of Christianese—complain about God's weather. That's right—all weather is ordained by God. God controls the weather. God is the sovereign One.

By God's grace, I want you to experience what I did years ago, that is, closure in my mind, once and for all, that God is sovereign over all of the weather. If He wants sun, rain, hail, sleet, or snow, then I will thank Him. The Old Testament name "God," in Hebrew, is "El-o-him" (not El Niño).

As Pink detailed, the Bible absolutely teaches that God, Elohim, is in absolute control of the weather. Ultimately, there are no "acts of nature" because all of nature obeys the very commands of Providence. The Reformer from Geneva, John Calvin, said, "It is certain that not one drop of rain falls without God's sure command."[3] God governs the sun, moon, rain, hail, snow, clouds, evaporation, wind, thunder, lightning, earthquakes, landslides, fire, ice, floods, and everything in between. He is the very Director of everything. Psalm 135:6–7 says,

> Whatever the LORD pleases, he does, in heaven and on earth, in the seas and all deeps. He it is who makes the clouds rise at the end of the earth, who makes lightnings for the rain and brings forth the wind from his storehouses.

What a far cry this is from Rabbi Kushner's bestseller *When Bad Things Happen to Good People*, where he argues that some things happen for no apparent reason. He thinks that when insurance companies consider fires, earthquakes, and tornados as "acts of God," that they are actually "...using God's name in vain!" Tragic thinking.

God is sovereign over creation and all things answer to Him. Psalm 119:90b–91 says, "You have established the earth, and it stands fast. By your appointment they stand this day, for all things are your servants." This also includes the weather. Did you know that the Bible rarely uses expressions like "it rains"? Rather, it almost always says that God sends the rain. Active voice. God sends.

God wants you to see the direct connection between the weather and His hand. For example:

> ...the LORD God had not caused it to rain on the land . . . (Genesis 2:5b)

> He will give the rain for your land in its season . . . (Deuteronomy 11:14)

---

[3]John Calvin, *Institutes of the Christian Religion*, volume 1, ed. John T. McNeill, translated and indexed by Ford Lewis Battles (Louisville, KY: Westminster John Knox Press, 1960, 2006), 201.

The LORD will open to you his good treasury, the heavens, to give the rain to your land in its season… (Deuteronomy 28:12a)

After many days the word of the LORD came to Elijah, in the third year, saying, "Go, show yourself to Ahab, and I will send rain upon the earth." (1 Kings 18:1)

Then I will give you your rains in their season, and the land shall yield its increase, and the trees of the field shall yield their fruit. (Leviticus 26:4)

The same thing goes for the wind. It is spoken of as coming from heaven itself:

For he commanded and raised the stormy wind, which lifted up the waves of the sea. He made the storm be still, and the waves of the sea were hushed. (Psalm 107:25–29)

Elohim even controls mildew and hail and they do only what He commands them to do:

I struck you and all the products of your toil with blight and with mildew and with hail, yet you did not turn to me, declares the LORD. (Haggai 2:17)

"I struck you with blight and mildew; your many gardens and your vineyards, your fig trees and your olive trees the locust devoured; yet you did not return to me," declares the LORD. (Amos 4:9)

The gigantic sun, as large and powerful as it is, is simply a miniature globe to God:

And the sun stood still, and the moon stopped, until the nation took vengeance on their enemies. Is this not written in the Book of Jashar? The sun stopped in the midst of heaven and did not hurry to set for about a whole day. (Joshua 10:13)

And Isaiah the prophet called to the LORD, and he brought the shadow back ten steps, by which it had gone down on the steps of Ahaz. (2 Kings 20:11)

"Behold, I will make the shadow cast by the declining sun on the dial of Ahaz turn back ten steps." So the sun turned back on the dial the ten steps by which it had declined. (Isaiah 38:8)

Commenting on these verses, Calvin said, "the sun does not daily rise and set by a blind instinct of nature but that of God Himself."[4] This truth is essential for the Christian. It will radically transform the proverbial complainer of the weather to a saint, reverently acknowledging God's good hand in everything.

Who is really in control of the weather? Does it really matter? How would this change your life, one way or another? Please answer this question tomorrow morning when you wake up and look out the window.

I will bless the LORD at all times; his praise shall continually be in my mouth. (Psalm 34:1)

Response

1. May you and every meteorologist proclaim the greatness of El-o-him, and His weather. If God has ordained rain or snow today, would arguing with God or submitting to Him be wiser?

2. Look at the weather from God's perspective. Viewing things from the correct angle renders the weather passive and God active.

Weather is like evolution. It is not controlled by anything, because it has no mind of its own. It is not its own, self-determining "thing" or "person." Weather is a term we use to describe what God does in nature when it comes to climate and climate differences. To be or not to be, that isn't the question. Weather isn't.

---

[4]Ibid., 199.

Chapter Eleven

. . .

White Lie #11: God Speaks Outside of His Revealed Word

. . .

When I was younger, much younger, my alarm clocks did not provide enough motivation to get out of bed. After my mother's patience wore thin, she would come to my room and say, "Mike, get up or you will get the 'water treatment.'" The dreaded but effective "water treatment." She would take water and sprinkle it on my face and neck. Flick. Soak. Annoy. Get up. This had nothing to do with modes or forms of Lutheran baptism; rather, it motivated me to get my lazy self out of bed.

God should have given sinful and rebellious humans the "silent treatment," but thankfully, because He is gracious, He did not. God speaks. God is a speaking God. God speaks to his creatures. God speaks to His sinful creatures.

While false idols have weight, form and mass, they are as mute as a piece of lava rock or cold marble. Silence is their tagline. Man-made idols, since they are nothing, offer only silence. We want to hear from our gods. We want to hear from God. "Speak to us" is every creature's desire from God. Every thinking person given one wish from God would request, "God, please speak to me."

Thankfully, God tells us what He thinks and how we are to think. To borrow from Francis Schaeffer's 1972 book title, *He Is There and He Is Not Silent*. While God silently teaches us about His power and wisdom through His creation (natural revelation), there are many things that the sun, moon, and stars cannot communicate. God must speak specifically so that we might understand things like Christ's life, death, resurrection, and soon return. You need a speaking God to know how to worship properly and grasp what God requires as a response to His work. You must have a "Thus says the LORD" God.

Secret Messages?

Speaking is one thing, but whispering and still small voices is another matter.

Does God regularly whisper special messages to His followers? Are they simply sweet nothings or are they real revelations? Should they be communicated? Written down? Added to Scripture? Inserted after Revelation? Does God walk with people and talk with people along life's narrow way? Does God still speak outside of His written Word?

Before we address the current evangelical trend of hearing from God outside of His Word, the story of a song will help us gain insight into the modern evangelical climate that desires more from God.

C. Austin Miles wrote "In the Garden" around 1912. Developing some film in his dark room, Miles imagined Mary Magdalene going to the empty tomb of Jesus. Furthermore, Miles claims he even "saw" Mary walk into a garden where he heard Jesus say, "Mary." After this experience, Miles immediately wrote the lyrics and then he later scored the music. "In the Garden" has been wildly popular ever since. Billy Sunday used the song at his crusades and Perry Como even recorded it in 1950. Miles relates the story:

> One day in April, 1912, I was seated in the dark room where I kept my photographic equipment, and also my organ. I drew my Bible toward me and it opened at my favorite book and chapter, John chapter twenty. I don't know if this was by chance or by the work of the Holy Spirit. I will let you the reader decide. That story of Jesus and Mary in John 20 had lost none of its power and charm.
>
> It was though I was in a trance, as I read it that day, I seemed to be part of the scene. I became a silent witness to that dramatic moment in Mary's life, when she knelt before her Lord and cried, "Rabboni." I rested my hands on the open Bible, as I stared at the light blue wall. As

the light faded, I seemed to be standing at the entrance of a garden, looking down a gently winding path, shaded by olive branches. A woman in white, with head bowed, hand clasping her throat, as if to choke back her sobs, walked slowly into the shadows. It was Mary. As she came unto the tomb, upon which she placed her hand, she bent over to look in, and ran away.

John, in a flowing robe, appeared looking at the tomb. Then came Peter, who entered the tomb, followed slowly by John. As they departed, Mary reappeared leaning her head upon her arm at the tomb, she wept. Turning herself, she saw Jesus standing there, so did I. I knew it was He. She knelt before Him, with arms outstretched, and looking into His face cried, "Rabboni."

I awakened in sunlight, gripping my Bible with my muscles tense, and nerves vibrating, under the inspiration of the Holy Spirit. I wrote as quickly as the words could be formed the lyrics exactly as it is sung today. That same evening, I wrote the tune. It is sung today as it was written in 1912.[1]

As we say in No Compromise Radio land, "Henno!" Did you notice how experience-driven the account was? When I first read the account I thought the only thing missing was some weird organ Muzak for accompaniment. I was "okay" with the dream until he said, "Under the inspiration of the Holy Spirit?" Then *my* muscles tensed and *my* nerves vibrated!

At least the story behind the song gives me new insight into the actual lyrics of the song. Now, "In the Garden" make perfect sense, even though it does not make biblical sense.

> I come to the garden alone
>
> While the dew is still on the roses
>
> And the voice I hear falling on my ear
>
> The Son of God discloses.

---

[1]Accessed from http://www.tanbible.com/tol_sng/sng_inthegarden.htm.

Refrain

And He walks with me, and He talks with me,

And He tells me I am His own;

And the joy we share as we tarry there,

None other has ever known.

He speaks, and the sound of His voice,

Is so sweet the birds hush their singing,

And the melody that He gave to me

Within my heart is ringing.

Refrain

I'd stay in the garden with Him

Though the night around me be falling,

But He bids me go; through the voice of woe

His voice to me is calling.[2]

If Mr. Miles really walked and actually talked with the real Jesus in a real garden, I am pretty sure that he would have fallen to his face in worship. Literally. Think Isaiah 6. Prostration. Undone. Woe is me! At best, the lyrics are sloppy and not very well nuanced. At worst, Miles is actually alleging new revelation. Strike that. He doesn't allege it, he claims it. Either way, Hebrews 1:1–4 is forgotten. Closed canons are opened. What does the Bible say about ongoing revelation? Hebrews 1 speaks clearly and concisely:

> Long ago, at many times and in many ways, God spoke to our fathers by the prophets, but in these last days he has spoken to us by his Son, whom he appointed the heir of all things, through whom also he created the world. He is the radiance of the glory of God and the exact imprint of his nature, and he upholds the universe by the word of his

---

[2]Accessed from http://cyberhymnal.org/htm/i/t/g/itgarden.htm.

power. After making purification for sins, he sat down at the right hand of the Majesty on high, having become as much superior to angels as the name he has inherited is more excellent than theirs. (Hebrews 1:1–4)

According to Hebrews 1, God has stopped giving new revelation. New revelation used to be given, but it stopped. While songwriters might "feel" inspired or claim to hear God, they are actually denying the sufficiency of Scripture and the first chapter of Hebrews. God used to speak through many ways. Dreams, audible voices and other subjective means of communication have ceased. Why? We are in "the last days," which is Bible-speak for the time period between Christ's first and second advent.

Can you spot the "white lie" in the following syllogism (syllogisms use propositional statements deductively to come to a reasoned conclusion):

1. God is immutable and does not change.

2. God used to speak.

3. Therefore, God speaks to us in the same way.

Let's break the syllogism down. God is a speaking God (so far so good). God is immutable and unchangeable (true). And then comes the conclusion that should even make a Star Wars Wookiee yelp, "Therefore, God still speaks today." Game. Set. Match. Winner, winner. Or maybe not. What is the problem with such "logic" ? "What are the problems?" might be a more accurate question. The major problem is that Hebrews 1:1–4 is not considered.

The theology of God's whispering today is everywhere. If you listen to Charles Stanley, as many people do, you would spot the wrong thinking if you paid careful attention. Stanley wrongly explains:

> Many people do not fully believe that God speaks today. If we think we get direction only through Scripture, then we miss out on much of what God has to share, because He will speak so often through His Spirit, circumstances, and other people. We must make absolutely certain that we are fully convinced and persuaded that God does speak to us personally...[3]

---

[3]Charles Stanley, *How to Listen to God* (Nashville, TN: Thomas Nelson, 1985), 128.

Miss out? Speak personally? Haves, meet the Have-nots. While Stanley certainly knows how to play on people's heartstrings, he tragically equates circumstances and other people with the Scriptures. Charles effectually elevates circumstances to the level of God's Word. David F. Wells encapsulates the argument:

> Granting the status of revelation to anything other than the Word of God inevitably has the effect of removing that status from the Word of God. What may start out as an additional authority alongside the Word of God will eventually supplant its authority altogether.[4]

Like it or not, God is done speaking. Case closed. Canon closed.

The Spirit and the Word

Let's try to approach this from a different angle. Today's charismatic has divorced the work of the Holy Spirit from the Word of God. They teach, essentially, that the Holy Spirit "talks" to them outside of and divorced from Scripture. Do not buy this "white lie." R.B. Kuiper's words are not only biblical and wise, but they are pungent. R.B. would have been a perfect No Compromise Radio guest with this provocative section of writing:

> It is of the essence of mysticism to separate the operation of the Holy Spirit from God's objective Word, to hold that the Spirit often reveals God's will without reference to the Bible, and thus by plain implication to deny that the Bible is God's once-for-all, finished revelation of his will.
>
> No student of Scripture will care to deny that before the Bible was completed God frequently revealed his will through such methods as visions, dreams, and the casting of lots. But to assert that God continues to do this after the completion of Holy Writ is to deny its sufficiency. That obviously is an extremely serious matter. And so we are not surprised to find the Westminster divines militat-

---

[4]David F. Wells, *God in the Wasteland* (Grand Rapids, MI: William B. Eerdmans, 1994), 109.

ing against it in the warning that nothing at any time is to be added to Scripture, not even "by new revelations of the Spirit."

And yet, how very prevalent is the notion that the will of God may be learned through special guidance of the Spirit, apart from the Word!

To claim special revelations of God's will by the Holy Spirit apart from Scripture sounds pious, but it is in reality wicked presumption, which lays him who makes the claim wide open to deception by Satan.[5]

Why are so many people prone to this "white lie?"[6]

While not exhaustive, I present four common reasons Christians fall prey to, what they perceive as, ongoing revelation. First, many folks are influenced by false teaching. Second, they are simply ignorant of what the Bible actually says about its sufficiency. They essentially mistake illumination with revelation. Third, they want more, and thereby demonstrate a certain level of discontentment with God for closing the canon. Fourth, people struggle with laziness.

Everyone struggles with laziness. Think about all that time it would take to learn Greek and Hebrew. Grammar, lexical studies, syntax, and historical considerations? Nah, don't need it because God speaks directly to me. Wow. Really?

What does Paul say to his protégé, Timothy?

Do your best to present yourself to God as one approved, a worker who has no need to be ashamed, rightly handling the word of truth. (2 Timothy 2:15)

Paul wants Timothy and every pastor and elder after him (and by implication, every Christian) to properly interpret and teach the Bible. But it takes work. Corners cannot be cut. Shortcuts must be avoided. Paul tells his young apprentice, using a Greek aorist impera-

---

[5]R.B. Kuiper, "Pitfalls in Finding God's Will for Your Life," accessed from http://www.opc.org/new_horizons/NH04/01b.html.

[6]Material from this section was taken from my book; Mike Abendroth, *Jesus Christ: The Prince of Preachers* (Leominster, UK: DayOne, 2007), 27–29. The author gave his permission.

tive, that he must not spare any effort in his study of the Bible. Proper Bible study is difficult (but rewarding). The word he uses means "do one's best, spare no effort, work hard."[7] The ESV's translation perfectly describes the requirement as "do your best." The lexicon BDAG defines it by saying, "to be especially conscientious in discharging an obligation, be zealous/eager, take pains, make every effort, be conscientious."[8] If this word meaning was not emphatic enough, the original language follows the word "do your best" with an infinitive to show the intensity of the command.[9] Paul wants church leaders to faithfully exert themselves in the loftiest of endeavors. Paul would have you to work hard as well. Do you begin to see why people are tempted to hear from God directly?

Furthermore, Timothy must present himself approved to God. The use of the second, singular, reflexive, pronoun leaves Timothy no option but to personally give an account of himself to God.[10] He must be the man to execute the imperative. No one likes to be shamed. "Shame on you" is not anyone's favorite thing to hear. Shame from others is one thing, but here Paul states that disobedience (lazy Bible study) would beget shame from God Himself. Gulp. The word "ashamed" "is passive; it does not merely mean 'unashamed,' but 'not forced to be ashamed,' namely by the fatal disapproval of God."[11] Human approval, gain, popularity, and money fade in the light of being shamed before and by God Himself. Talk about motivation to dig into the text! The term "worker" points not to the needed skill in the performance of his task but to the laboriousness involved in its execution. The effort is described as an "exhausting toil."[12]

How much work does it entail to "hear sweet whispers from God?" Why aren't there commands in the Bible designed to help the readers

---

[7]Barclay M. Newman, A Concise Greek-English Dictionary of the New Testament [CD- ROM] (United Bible Societies), in Bible Works (Norfolk, VA: BibleWorks LLC, 1992–2003), s.v., "spoudazo."

[8]BDAG, s.v., "spoudazo."

[9]George Knight weighs in saying, "This imperative intensifies the command expressed by the infinitive clause that it governs." Commentary on the Pastoral Epistles, 411.

[10]Knight, Commentary on the Pastoral Epistles, 411.

[11]R.C.H. Lenski, The Interpretation of St. Paul's Epistles to the Colossians, to the Thessalonians, to Timothy, to Titus and to Philemon (Minneapolis, MN: Augsburg Publishing House, 1937, 1946), 798.

[12]D. Edmond Hiebert, Second Timothy (Chicago, IL: Moody, 1958), 67–68.

decipher words from the Lord? There are no commands because they are not needed since the canon of Scripture is now closed. God is no longer speaking outside of His revealed Word. If the Charismatics were right, one would think that Timothy might be told, "Do your best to rightly divide the impressions, words from God, or still small voices." After all, if God is speaking, you had better interpret Him rightly![13]

What does this work imply? Timothy must accurately handle the word of God by interpreting it properly. It literally means "cutting straight."[14] The question is "what does 'cutting straight' mean?" This word is somewhat controversial, but "Recent reference works and commentaries tend to agree that the cutting imagery is less important than the idea of correctness."[15] BDAG elaborates: "It…plainly means 'cut a path in a straight direction' or 'cut a road across country (that is forested or otherwise difficult to pass through) in a straight direction,' so that the traveler may go directly to his destination."[16] The Word needs to be rightly divided. Impressions are simply impressions, so work is necessary. Impressions are not revelation from God. So treat them as what they are. And aren't.

This positive command also warns against handling the Word wrongly. Hendricksen says the man who is obedient to Paul is "the man who handles the word of the truth properly [and] does not change, pervert, mutilate, or distort it, neither does he use it with a wrong purpose in mind."[17] Accuracy and truthfulness are the goal of the teacher. He is to be in stark opposition to Elymas the magician, of whom Scripture says,

> But Elymas the magician (for that is the meaning of his name) opposed them, seeking to turn the proconsul away from the faith. But Saul, who was also called Paul, filled with the Holy Spirit, looked intently at him and said, "You son of the devil, you enemy of all righteousness, full

---

[13]What is missing in the Pastoral Epistles (1 Timothy, 2 Timothy and Titus)? Conspicuous by its absence is any direction for understanding new revelation. Paul knew the canon was closing and, therefore, did not need to give his protégé pointers on discerning true from false revelation.

[14]*Thayer's Lexicon* [CD-ROM], in Bible Works (Norfolk, VA: BibleWorks LLC, 1992– 2003), s.v. *"orthotomounta."*

[15]Walter L. Liefeld, *1 and 2 Timothy, Titus,* The NIV Application Commentary, ed. Terry Muck (Grand Rapids, MI: Zondervan, 1999), 258.

[16]BDAG, s.v. *"orthotomounta."*

[17]Hendricksen, *I-II Timothy and Titus,* 263.

of all deceit and villainy, will you not stop making crooked the straight paths of the Lord?" (Acts 13:8–10)

The preacher must lay down a trail for others, so that they might follow it. You are now on that path. Just like the pastor or teacher, you must understand the Bible correctly, and that means you must first properly understand and interpret the Bible. Unlike understanding impressions, Bible study takes work. Lots of it. Don't opt for the lazy route. Some say, "We must study the Scriptures to see if our impressions match up with the Word." Why? If the impressions agree with the Bible, you don't need the impressions because you have the Bible.

Paul stresses the importance of the clear and true teaching charge when he describes Scripture as "the word of truth." Knight explains it by saying, "The sense of the phrase here is probably best conveyed in the rendering 'message of the truth.' To handle the word correctly is to handle it in accord with its intention and to communicate properly its meaning."[18] Who needs all this work when the Lord whispers to us privately and personally? Henno.

Missionary Jonathan Goforth (a great name for a missionary) epitomizes a person who is committed to study the revealed Word of God. He stated, "My deepest regret, on reaching threescore years and ten, is that I have not devoted more time to the study of the Bible. Still in less than nineteen years I have gone through the New Testament in Chinese fifty-five times."[19] King David similarly wrote, "More to be desired are they than gold, even much fine gold; sweeter also than honey and drippings of the honeycomb" (Psalm 19:10).

I am not saying that all Charismatics are lazy. Well, yes I am. Cessationists and Charismatics both struggle with laziness. What am I saying? Apart from the exegetical arguments, don't opt for the easy way, especially since the easy way is the wrong way. It will take you down a detour named "White Lie Boulevard."

More Sinister?

There is another matter to ponder in this debate—many people want God to talk like a lover. A physical lover. I wish I did not have to type that last sentence fragment. Personally. Privately. With whispers. Of course, Jesus is the lover of our souls. Of course, Jesus loves us with

---

[18]Knight, *Commentary on the Pastoral Epistles*, 412.

[19]Accessed from http://www.wholesomewords.org/missions/msrevival.html.

an everlasting love. Of course, God's love for us will never cease. Of course! But Jesus talks to both men and women in the same fashion. Re-read that last sentence. This is obvious because both men and women have the same 66 books of the Bible. But if you think that revelation still comes fast and furiously, you have to have a reason. My hunch is that many ladies want a lover-Jesus to "talk to them." How do I know that there are many who hanker for this? Answer: Jesus Calling, by Sarah Young. If you like her book, you have major problems. If you are a man and like her book, you might be beyond help. Almost.

Sarah has tapped into a yearning and a longing, but she is tragically and biblically mistaken. The problem is that modern evangelicals have such little discernment—they have purchased enough copies of this book to fill the Mariana Trench.

When you sell more books than Stephen King, you have met a felt need. You have scratched an itch. The book's Amazon page boldly asserts:

> Jesus Calling is a devotional filled with uniquely inspired treasures from heaven for every day of the year. After many years of writing in her prayer journal, missionary Sarah Young decided to listen to God with pen in hand, writing down whatever she believed He was saying to her. It was awkward at first, but gradually her journaling changed from monologue to dialogue. She knew her writings were not inspired as Scripture is, but journaling helped her grow closer to God. Others were blessed as she shared her writings, until people all over the world were using her messages.[20]

The publisher's "Product Description" tells me everything I need to know about Sarah's mysticism:

> After many years of writing her own words in her prayer journal, missionary Sarah Young decided to be more attentive to the Savior's voice and begin listening for what He was saying. So with pen in hand, she embarked on a journey that forever changed her—and many others around the world. In these powerful pages are the words and Scriptures Jesus lovingly laid on her heart. Words of

---

[20]Accessed from http://www.amazon.com/Jesus-Calling-Enjoying-Peace-Presence/dp/1591451884/ref=sr_1_1?ie=UTF8&qid=1454529988&sr=8-1&keywords=jesus+calling.

reassurance, comfort, and hope. Words that have made her increasingly aware of His presence and allowed her to enjoy His peace.

Call me a crusty cessationist, but I don't like it when people say they hear from God outside of His Word, but I pretty much go apopletic when people say they speak for God. What blasphemy. What treachery. What nonsense.

When people are not satisfied with God's Word (and by the way, there is a whole lot of Bible to study), nothing will satisfy them. It won't take long before their "Sarah's version of Jesus" breeds a spirit of malcontent. Listen to Sarah's own words and see if you spot the lack of contentment (it isn't difficult):

> I began to wonder if I, too, could receive messages during my times of communing with God. I had been writing in prayer journals for years, but that was one-way communication: I did all the talking. I knew that God communicated with me through the Bible, *but I yearned for more. Increasingly, I wanted to hear what God had to say to me personally on a given day.* I decided to listen to God with pen in hand, writing down whatever I believed He was saying. (emphasis added)[21]

Mark it—Jesus NEVER talked to Sarah. Ever. God's Word is sufficient and enough. One entry from Sarah's Jesus should be enough for you to run and find one of my grandmother's homemade remedies for gurgly stomachs:

> January 8: Softly I announce my Presence. Shimmering hues of radiance tap gently at your consciousness, seeking entrance. Though I have all Power in heaven and on earth, I am infinitely tender with you. The weaker you are, the more gently I approach you. Let your weakness be a door to My Presence. Whenever you feel inadequate, remember that I am your *ever-present Help.* Hope in Me, and you will be protected from depression and self-pity. Hope is like a golden cord connecting you to heaven. The more you cling to this cord, the more I bear the weight of your burdens; thus, you are lightened. Heaviness is not of My

---

[21]Sarah Young, *Jesus Calling: Enjoying Peace in His Presence* (Nashville, TN: Thomas Nelson, 2004, 2011, 2012), xiii.

kingdom. Cling to hope, and My rays of Light will reach you through the darkness. Psalm 46:1; Romans 12:12; Romans 15:13.[22]

If what Sarah said is biblical, which it is not, then there is no reason for God to say it again. If what Sarah said is unbiblical, which it is, then it isn't from God.

Watch out!

Jonathan Edwards has some good advice that Sarah Young followers need to heed yesterday. Edwards writes, "As long as a person has a notion that he is guided by immediate direction from heaven, it makes him incorrigible and impregnable in all his misconduct."[23]

---

[22]Ibid., 9.

[23]Jonathan Edwards, *The Works of Jonathan Edwards*, vol. 1 (London: William Ball, 1839), 404.

Chapter Twelve

, , ,

White Lie #12: Bible Characters Make Perfect Models for Morality

, , ,

Flannelgraphs, alternatively named flannel boards, are sturdy panels covered with flannel. Duh. Displayed on an easel, they facilitate the telling of stories, usually in the small nooks and crannies of basements (called "classrooms") in many Christian church buildings. While most basements reek of semi-sanctified mold and tater-tot casseroles, flannelgraphs are impervious to the odor. Flannel representations of Bible characters are also versatile and easy to manufacture. Think visual. Cutout Bible characters easily adhere to the flannel background, making an inexpensive but memorable story time for children of most ages. I can still picture, and even feel, Daniel and the lion's den, Esther before the king, fiery furnaces, Moses and his staff, and a donkey who supposedly talked (flannelgraphs don't bray, kick, or actually speak). Every week the thin flannel delivered an exciting and wonderful story. But was that it? Was it just a simple story? Or was it supposed to be more?

Beyond the Flannel Veil

Most stories can be illustrated with cut-out characters or probably even with Jell-O® molds. 3-D might be more impressive, but cost undoubtedly rises in direct relationship to impressibility and the additional dimension. If the storyteller has a clue, even non-ambulatory "Moses" figures seem to come alive when plastered next to a cutout piece of flannel representing a burning bush that does not burn. But it is hard to illustrate abstract thoughts with flannel, clay, or any other tangible substance. While flannel might bring the stories of the destruction of Sodom and

Gomorrah to life for young folks, they do not capture the smoky, sulfuric odor very well, nor do they incorporate the Christ-centered, redemptive theme that is found throughout the entire Old Testament (and certainly the New Testament as well).

Old Testament stories, told with or without flannel, need to be related to the Messiah and His redemptive plan. In one fashion or another, all biblical stories need to be shown as part of the grand sweep and swath of progressive revelation. A revelation that ultimately points to Jesus. Do you remember that Jesus set Himself as the centerpiece at the table of the Old Testament?

> Then he said to them, "These are my words that I spoke to you while I was still with you, that everything written about me in the Law of Moses and the Prophets and the Psalms must be fulfilled." (Luke 24:44)

In the grand picture of salvation, every aspect of the Old Testament weaves itself as one fabric showing Jesus Christ. Jesus, using the tri-fold designation of the Old Testament to emphasize comprehensiveness, taught that all of the Old Testament preaches Christ the Messiah. The Old Testament is a Christian testament. The Old Testament is mainly about Jesus. Jesus not only is the fulfillment of the Old Testament, but He is the theme, the focus and the subject matter. In fact, Jesus emphatically declared that the Old Testament was bearing witness of Him:

> You search the Scriptures because you think that in them you have eternal life; and it is they that bear witness about me, yet you refuse to come to me that you may have life. (John 5:39–40)

While scholars differ on the degree of seeing Christ in the Old Testament, it is not argued that He is prominently found from Genesis to Malachi (or 2 Chronicles in the Hebrew canon). But how do you portray Christ in the Old Testament on a flannelgraph? Should every Old Testament flannel story kit come custom-stocked with a Jesus figure? Should a flannel Jesus (I guess He might have a beard and longer hair, but then, who did not in those days?) be plastered on, over, or next to Esther, Elijah, and Eli? Can't you see a child-attached Jesus hovering above Joseph's dungeon, almost like a UFO? How is Jesus to be incorporated into every scene so that Luke 24:44 and John 5:39–40 are accurately represented?

The "white lie" is not a lie of addition; it is the lack of it. Don't forget the entire story. Don't forget Jesus. Don't teach moralistic stories using biblical characters. If your goal was moralism, why not use Aesop's Fables? Avoid the "white lie" by teaching narratives in context. Christians are pretty good at noticing the immediate context of a passage, especially New Testament Epistles. Many evangelicals err when they forget the context of the particular story in light of the entire Bible (a wider context)—God's grand theme of redemption.

So that the cutouts stick to the flannel background, flannelgraph characters were also made of flannel, fuzzy felt, or were backed with sandpaper so they would not fall into fiery furnaces prematurely—or plunge headfirst onto linoleum floors with unmatched patterns (since they were donated to the church, and free is free). Jesus and sandpaper? Sounds more like something John the Baptist would wear. We know flannel can stick to honey, but can it adhere to locusts? Getting the narrative to stick in the minds of the children may be relatively easy, but how can flannel demonstrate the story of the Redeemer and adequately represent Christ in an Old Testament narrative, poem, or prophecy? I am glad you asked. How can we teach the Old Testament while keeping authorial intent and showing the grand theme of redemption?

A Case Study

Let's examine the book of Ruth and the lady named Ruth so that we can discover whether or not woolly cloth can hold its Christological own with this Old Testament treasure.

Ruth?

When a book is entitled "Ruth," the reader really cannot be blamed if he mentally props up the name of the book as the central figure. I am not actually advocating changing the name of the book, but for the sake of mental highlighting I want you to add Boaz to the title of the book of Ruth. But you need to add more than Boaz. The theological subtitle to Ruth should be: Christ is a personal redeemer like Boaz, but better. If you still insist on Ruth in the book's title, how about "Ruth's redemption through Christ-like Boaz" or "God's Majestic Sovereignty as a Boaz-like Redeemer in Ruth's life and lineage?" Catchy? Popular? Flannel worthy?

Some books of the Bible received their names due to a predominant theme unfolding throughout. For example, Genesis is a book of beginnings, and Exodus stresses Israel's physical redemption from Egypt. Psalms contains psalms, or songs, and the book of Proverbs teaches wisdom through sayings. Occasionally, the moniker of the book is based on its author. James wrote James and Peter wrote 1 Peter and 2 Peter. Other books were letters named after the people they were meant to address (Hebrews, Romans, Philemon, etc.). Lastly, there are a few books, like Samuel and Job, which relate stories about their namesakes. The book of Ruth correctly conveys the idea that the letter is about this particular lady, but is Ruth the character of characters throughout these four chapters? Should the name of Ruth be Ruth?

Ruth, the woman, could and should be commended at many levels. Some of her positive attributes could include:

- Converting from paganism to Judaism (Ruth 1:16)
- Showing loyalty to her mother-in-law (Ruth 1:16–17)
- Being in the royal line of David (Ruth 4:18–22)
- Devotion in the dark days of Judges
- Supporting her mother-in-law (Ruth 2)
- Humility (Ruth 2:10–13)
- Hard worker (Ruth 2:7)
- Sacrificing food for the sake of Naomi (Ruth 2:14, 18)
- Seen by Boaz as having outstanding character (Ruth 3:10)

For a Gentile, Ruth isn't too shabby and definitely flannel worthy. She is admirable in many ways and, in a strictly moral world, is a person to imitate. But is that the author's intention? Is the purpose of this book to teach someone to "be like Ruth?" Let's not rush to such a verdict. Be careful—when the author's intention is overlooked, kooky and often bizarre lessons are both forcibly extracted from and wrongly imposed upon the Old Testament. I think I could convince you if I asked, "What would you say if someone taught Ruth as an example of how to get along with a difficult mother-in-law?" Or used Ruth to highlight the practical advantages of sleeping at the feet of a man, especially after he has eaten and had a few drinks ("How to get an eligible bachelor")? We readily refuse these applications. Bravo.

Does the Book of Ruth mainly teach its readers to imitate Ruth? Follow Ruth? Ruth is only who she is because of another's redemption! Without the Lord's grace, Ruth would be doing what was right in her own eyes just like the rest of the people living at the time of the Judges (Ruth 1:1). Admittedly, Ruth is the great-grandmother of David (Ruth

4:22), who is in the royal line of Jesus, but is the book of Ruth primarily about Ruth the woman? While Ruth the lady should not be denigrated, the reader of the book of Ruth needs unclouded vision to see past Ruth as the key person in the narrative. Daniel Block concurs, "Ruth is not the main character of the book…of the 3 main actors in the drama, however, Ruth speaks the least often, and her speeches are the shortest."[1] So Ruth should be out of the running for the book name and the primary flannel character. Ruth does not redeem. *Ruth receives redemption.*

Naomi?

Everyone would agree that Naomi would be a poor choice for the title of the biblical book we call, Ruth. Naomi was often manipulative, angry, sullen, and a poor example of an Israelite. If the Old Testament simply contained examples (and it includes much more than that, hence this book), she would go down in history as a wonderful illustration (drum roll) of what not to do! Naomi's mini résumé in Ruth:

- Insist that your daughter-in-law stay among pagan people (Ruth 1:15)

- Blame God for one's suffering (Ruth 1:13, 20–21)

- Bitterly respond to the providence of God (Ruth 1:13)

- Be a real downer upon returning to the Promised Land (Ruth 1:19 ff.)

- Push Ruth to initiate a wedding proposal (instead of doing it herself) (Ruth 3:3–4)

- Plan a rather sensual approach to a possible wedding (Ruth 3:3–7)

- Place daughter-in-law into a dangerous position (Ruth 3:7–8)

It seems obvious that Naomi also is disqualified as a contender for book title and primary flannel character. It is important to recognize, though, that she does understand the redeemer concept and surely taught Ruth about Yahweh while they both were in Moab. Yet, sour and glowering are hard to depict in flannel, unless you resort to a Batman-like cartoon slogan (remember those? "Whack!" "Kapow!") that says "Crabby" or "Grumpy."

---

[1]Daniel I. Block, *Judges, Ruth: An Exegetical and Theological Exposition of Holy Scripture*, in New American Commentary (Nashville, TN: Holman Reference, 1999), 588.

Boaz?

Boaz, aside from having what might be the coolest name of all time, was a man of wealth, integrity, and nobility. The book of Ruth portrays him as an ethically upright man in a slimy and decadent world. Boaz's character shines forth as:

- Generous (Ruth 2:8–16)
- Compassionate (Ruth 3:11–13)
- Fatherly (Ruth 2:8, 3:10)
- Just (Ruth 3:12–13, 4:11)
- Godly (Ruth 3:10, 4:11)
- Sacrificial (Ruth 3:7–12)

But slow down, reader. Don't be tempted to do to Boaz what we tempered ourselves against regarding Ruth—making her, or him, central. Do not skirt Luke 24 and John 5. At all costs, avoid glomming onto Boaz as a means of highlighting social justice and welfare (since he allows Ruth to work for food so that she does not need to accept handouts).

Yet, in Boaz' life, isn't there stress on a man who redeems? A relative who rescues and provides? Boaz is more than a flicker of a sacrificial redeemer. Boaz shouts a truth. Boaz points to a greater Boaz. What kind of man redeems even a Moabite woman? If brown is the new black, then when it comes to Bible books, Boaz is the new Ruth. But the kinsman redeemer is illustrative of the greater Kinsman Redeemer. Remember, the Old Testament bears witness to Jesus. Boaz is a pointer, not the destination.

Four Flannel-Defying Truths

Think about the lunacy of the following illustration. A classroom of children watches flannelgraphic representations of stalks of grain, sand, and Middle Eastern looking people, but the teacher never describes them. The teacher is mute and basically allows the children to interpret the figures for themselves. Postmodern? Sounds like it. Abstract methods that would make Andy Warhol proud? Probably. Dumb? Oh yes, literally dumb. Figurines need words to be understood. How much more do abstract thoughts need words? Imagine a Sunday school teacher who would not speak while they were using the flannelgraph. Mime Sundays? Imagine a Christian Sunday school teacher who would not discuss the Messiah? Sadly, in light of the plethora of moralistic Vacation Bible School curricula and ideologies, one need not imagine this even for a nanosecond because they are seemingly everywhere.

Today, many insist that they are strictly visual learners, but God teaches both by sight in natural revelation (Romans 1:20–21) and also by special revelation, which is His written Word. Abstract spiritual truths need explanations. What is a word worth? If you only use a flannelgraph, the students miss out on the most important truths in the book of Ruth. I would not deny that Sunday school teachers actually talk and use words while utilizing flannelgraphs, but if those teachers forget to tie the Old Testament characters to the redemptive theme of the Bible, they remain essentially mute. To lower the volume on the promised Redeemer of Genesis 3:15 and Genesis 12 is to deafen the reader to the sight of God's plan of redemption.

Put another way, Jewish rabbis might affirm flannel stories of Ruth, but they should not agree with the teacher who rightly and ultimately directs the student to the Messiah, Jesus Christ, and the thread of redemption through the Abrahamic Covenant. Words that do not include a discussion of the Messiah are just as silent as flannel even if they are softer than the flannel itself.

In 1987, President Ronald Reagan bellowed, "Mr. Gorbachev, tear down this wall" as he verbally confronted the Russian government and insisted that they destroy the Berlin Wall. While I am not advocating perpetrating physical violence on flannelgraph easels, I do wish to rid "Christian" churches of every "-ism," including moralism and heroism, so that Jesus is preeminent in all Bible teaching, including the Old Testament (1 Corinthians 2:2). Tear down the flannel wall if doing so links the Old Testament story to the Messiah and to God's redeeming character.

The following four critical truths require words, thoughts, and concepts.[2] These truths require Jesus' words in Luke 24 to be taken seriously. These are four ways the book of Ruth preaches Christ.

1. Ruth *the Moabite* (points to CHRIST):

I am not sure how differently Jewish people looked compared to the Moabites. How would a flannelgraph depict the difference between Naomi and Ruth's skin tone and color? How could enhanced stick figures

---

[2]These truths could be verbally added to any flannelgraph presentation!

stress what the author emphasizes with the haunting and ceaseless refrain, "Ruth the Moabitess"? Moabites were gross and wicked. Moabites worshiped the reprehensible god Chemosh. Reverence to an angry, murderous, destroying fish god is never admirable. But in a revolting way, the origin of the Moabites towers over the false god they served. I dare you to read the following without wincing, cringing, or looking over your shoulder:

> Now Lot went up out of Zoar and lived in the hills with his two daughters, for he was afraid to live in Zoar. So he lived in a cave with his two daughters. And the firstborn said to the younger, "Our father is old, and there is not a man on earth to come in to us after the manner of all the earth. Come, let us make our father drink wine, and we will lie with him, that we may preserve offspring from our father." So they made their father drink wine that night. And the firstborn went in and lay with her father. He did not know when she lay down or when she arose. The next day, the firstborn said to the younger, "Behold, I lay last night with my father. Let us make him drink wine tonight also. Then you go in and lie with him, that we may preserve offspring from our father." So they made their father drink wine that night also. And the younger arose and lay with him, and he did not know when she lay down or when she arose. Thus both the daughters of Lot became pregnant by their father. The firstborn bore a son and called his name Moab. He is the father of the Moabites to this day. (Genesis 19:30–37)

The earlier lessons Lot taught his daughters were implemented in that dark, shameful cave. Who needs godliness and propriety when pragmatic needs are real? Lot was willing to hand over his daughters to the men in Genesis 19:8, so incest must not have been viewed as a significant issue either. The ends justified the means, and the repulsive Moabites were hatched. Remember the cave.

Ruth 1:3–4, with narrative understatement, states that the Jewish boys married Moabite wives. Ruth was a Moabite and the author does not wish for the reader to forget that shocking fact. Listen to the refrain with the cave of Genesis 19 ruminating in your soul (emphasis added):

So Naomi returned, and *Ruth the Moabite*, her daughter-in-law with her, who returned from the country of Moab. And they came to Bethlehem at the beginning of barley harvest. (Ruth 1:22)

And *Ruth the Moabite* said to Naomi, "Let me go to the field and glean among the ears of grain after him in whose sight I shall find favor." And she said to her, "Go, my daughter." (Ruth 2:2)

And the servant who was in charge of the reapers answered, "She is the young *Moabite woman*, who came back with Naomi from the country of Moab." (Ruth 2:6)

And *Ruth the Moabite* said, "Besides, he said to me, 'You shall keep close by my young men until they have finished all my harvest.'" (Ruth 2:21)

Then Boaz said, "The day you buy the field from the hand of Naomi, you also acquire *Ruth the Moabite*, the widow of the dead, in order to perpetuate the name of the dead in his inheritance." (Ruth 4:5)

Also *Ruth the Moabite*, the widow of Mahlon, I have bought to be my wife, to perpetuate the name of the dead in his inheritance, that the name of the dead may not be cut off from among his brothers and from the gate of his native place. You are witnesses this day. (Ruth 4:10)

Ruth is important because the reader sees God's love for pagans like her. As an object of God's favor, Ruth must be grasped. Bible students should be amazed at the inclusive aspect of the Messiah's redeeming love. God loves Moabites. Did you catch that? *God loves Moabites*. Gentiles. Are you a Gentile? Are you thankful that God's grace in Christ Jesus reaches to sinners, ungodly, enemies, and the helpless (Romans 5:6–11)? From incest to the Davidic line—could anything but God's condescending love explain such a turn of events? Who but Jesus Himself could turn a dark dungeon of a cave into a bright and beaming light of salvation and sanctification?

If we could go to heaven and ask Ruth if she would mind people looking past her to the Redeemer, how do you think she would reply? Could you explain *that* with a piece of flannel?

2. Genealogy (points to CHRIST):

Flannelgraph: The Genealogy Series. Not a bestseller, even if it were a sequel. All the cut-outs seem to look the same. Fuzzy. Olive skin. Middle Eastern look. Repeat. Not too tall. Not too short. Just right.

One of the errors in reading the book of Ruth is that some people forget to read the book in one sitting. While I love expository preaching, there are times when this type of delivery can divide the book into pieces and detract from the whole story. The end of Ruth is actually the beginning. Ruth must be read all at once. The book of Ruth pushes and drives toward the climax of the story. Just before "The End," we read:

> Now these are the generations of Perez: Perez fathered Hezron, Hezron fathered Ram, Ram fathered Amminadab, Amminadab fathered Nahshon, Nahshon fathered Salmon, Salmon fathered Boaz, Boaz fathered Obed, Obed fathered Jesse, and Jesse fathered David. (Ruth 4:18–22)

Why list the genealogy at the end of Ruth? Leon Morris writes:

> It is an interesting fact that though David is the greatest king spoken of in the historical books, and though he is looked on by subsequent generations as the ideal king, there is no genealogy of him in I Samuel. There he is simply "the son of Jesse." The book of Ruth closes with a genealogy running back to Pharez, the son of Judah. It is suggested that the book was written to supply the missing genealogy.[3]

Kings need genealogies so that they are considered legitimate. Yet if ever a group of people should be deemed "illegitimate," it must be the Moabites. To be fathered out of wedlock pales in respect to incest initiated by daughters. Thus, in society and in Jewish culture, Ruth is illegitimate.

Who could have imagined that David would descend from Boaz and Ruth? Boaz, yes, but Ruth? But God! But God! Amazingly, Ruth is included in the scriptural family tree of Matthew's Gospel:

> The book of the genealogy of Jesus Christ, the son of David, the son of Abraham. Abraham was the father of Isaac,

---

[3]Leon Morris, *Ruth: An Introduction and Commentary: Judges Ruth* (Downers Grove, IL: Inter-Varsity Press, 1973 [reprint]), 241.

and Isaac the father of Jacob, and Jacob the father of Judah and his brothers, and Judah the father of Perez and Zerah by Tamar, and Perez the father of Hezron, and Hezron the father of Ram, and Ram the father of Amminadab, and Amminadab the father of Nahshon, and Nahshon the father of Salmon, and Salmon the father of Boaz by Rahab, and Boaz the father of Obed by *Ruth*, and Obed the father of Jesse, and Jesse the father of David the king. And David was the father of Solomon by the wife of Uriah. (Matthew 1:1–6, emphasis added)

The ultimate King David, Jesus Christ, the Lord of Lords and King of Kings, comes via the ancestry of Boaz and Ruth. The lineage of Jesus contains Moabite blood. Not even a transparent flannel board could show such a blessed truth! Matthew says that you cannot understand Jesus without grasping Abraham and then he goes on to say the same thing of Ruth.

Jesus identified with sinners. Jesus ate with sinners. Jesus ministered to sinners. Jesus forgave sinners. Jesus' family tree was populated with sinners. Jesus descended from sinners. Jesus died a sinner's death. And all of these, yet Jesus was holy, blameless, and not a sinner. Jesus was the sinless second Adam and perfectly obeyed the Father. Could sinners be forgiven if Jesus had died at the feet of sadistic Herod? If Jesus had been massacred with the rest of the male children under two, would heaven be open for sinners? No, because Jesus needed to live a life of obedience in the place of sinners. Listen to Paul:

> But when the fullness of time had come, God sent forth his Son, born of woman, born under the law, to redeem those who were under the law, so that we might receive adoption as sons. And because you are sons, God has sent the Spirit of his Son into our hearts, crying, "Abba! Father!" So you are no longer a slave, but a son, and if a son, then an heir through God. (Galatians 4:4–7)

Preach the representative Jesus from Ruth!

3.   Providence (points to CHRIST):

Most Christians can hardly observe God's providence in their own lives let alone on a flannel backdrop with a small, yellow disk representing the sun and some brown ground representing the sand and dirt of

Moab. A tumbleweed here and a goat there. Providence is invisible because God is invisible. God exists and God works, but like the wind, only the effects of His work can be seen and understood by humans.

Christians regularly hanker for miracles, signs, and wonders when they should be reflecting on the nature and scope of God's providential workings in history, which includes their very own lives. Providence seems oblique and dark when looking into the future. We only know God will be in our future with His grace, but we do not know the twists and turns that the Sovereign Lord ordains. Often circuitous, usually sprinkled with difficulty, God extols His glory in time and has the believer's good in mind. In that order. Providence becomes clear looking backwards in time. Observe God's dealings with you. See God in Ruth. Aha! I see.

The hero of the Bible has always been Jesus. What does Ruth teach us about Jesus? How does Ruth point to Christ the Lord? Ruth is not important for who she is intrinsically, but for whom God arranges for her to providentially meet. Keith Mathison illustrates the providential workings of God in Ruth, saying:

> Whereas the book of Judges portrays the nation of Israel in an almost exclusively negative light, the book of Ruth indicates that covenant faithfulness did continue to exist during these years and that in the midst of this time of turmoil God was providentially preparing to raise up a king . . . God is providentially preparing the family through whom David will come. As part of his preparations for the monarchy, God extends his blessings to a Gentile Moabite woman and brings her into the covenant community. Among the descendants of this Moabite woman will be her great-grandson David, and ultimately Jesus himself (Matt. 1:5–6). The book of Ruth clearly teaches that God has not forsaken Israel during this time of widespread apostasy, and he has not forgotten his promises.[4]

An infinite amount of flannel could not unveil the truths of God that Mathison describes from Ruth. God is sovereignly working because God is supreme and He is immutable. It should not take long for the reader to figure out that God is working in the days of the Judges. Ruth's narrative regularly punctuates God's involvement in the lives of people:

---

[4]Keith Mathison, *From Age to Age* (Phillipsburg, PA: P & R, 2009), 90–91.

Would you therefore wait till they were grown? Would you therefore refrain from marrying? No, my daughters, for it is exceedingly bitter to me for your sake that the hand of the LORD has gone out against me. (Ruth 1:13)

She said to them, "Do not call me Naomi; call me Mara, for the Almighty has dealt very bitterly with me. I went away full, and the LORD has brought me back empty. Why call me Naomi, when the LORD has testified against me and the Almighty has brought calamity upon me?" (Ruth 1:20–21)

The LORD repay you for what you have done, and a full reward be given you by the LORD, the God of Israel, under whose wings you have come to take refuge! (Ruth 2:12)

Then all the people who were at the gate and the elders said, "We are witnesses. May the LORD make the woman, who is coming into your house, like Rachel and Leah, who together built up the house of Israel. May you act worthily in Ephrathah and be renowned in Bethlehem, and may your house be like the house of Perez, whom Tamar bore to Judah, because of the offspring that the LORD will give you by this young woman." (Ruth 4:11–12)

God is sovereignly working and controlling every event in the lives of the people in the book of Ruth. The only way the reader can recognize "invisible" providence is because the writer supplies the details of God's total control. Even the word, "LORD," or *Yahweh*, is listed 17 times in Ruth (*Elohim* is used only three times and *Shaddai* is found twice), signifying God's living and active presence in the lives of His covenant people. God superintends Boaz to redeem all because of the Messiah's redemption. God rules over redemption. Peter highlighted the Messiah's preexistence in 1 Peter 1:20–21, "He was foreknown before the foundation of the world but was made manifest in the last times for the sake of you who through him are believers in God, who raised him from the dead and gave him glory, so that your faith and hope are in God." Looking back, we understand that God, in eternity past, always had the plan to send the Son. It makes sense that such an eternal plan would pop up regularly and often in redemptive history.

God's kind providence is so prominent in Ruth that it nearly over-shadows the need for a kinsman-redeemer. Close, but not quite. Do you know where to buy any invisible pieces of flannel?

4.   Redeemer (or Kinsman-Redeemer) (points ultimately to CHRIST):

Boaz preaches the qualities of Jesus Christ. Everyone agrees that Boaz was not actually Jesus. Boaz was just a man, not the God-man. Boaz needed redemption because he was a sinner. But the writer of Ruth makes the reader see Christ painted in the portrait of Boaz. He saves. He is the kinsman-redeemer. He rescues. Who is "He?" Boaz or Jesus? Yes! David Murray wisely instructs of Ruth, "The book might equally be named after him because he is the center and pivot of the book. Chapter 1 begins with a bitter Naomi, and the book ends with a blessed Naomi. What made the difference? Three chapters of Boaz. All eyes should be on him."[5]

God promised to Adam and Eve that He Himself would provide a Messiah. Genesis 3:15 states, "I will put enmity between you and the woman, and between your offspring and her offspring; he shall bruise your head, and you shall bruise his heel." Wonderful! But what are the specifics? What will the coming Savior be like? The Jews understood that God is a redeeming God because of the deliverance out of Egypt, but could there be more that is known? How does God redeem? God powerfully redeems, but is there a personal aspect to God's redemption? God redeems nations, but does He redeem individual sinners? Jesus is like Boaz, but better! David Murray insightfully highlights the big picture:

> The key word in the book also dramatically spotlights Boaz. The Hebrew word ga'al appears twelve times and the noun version of it nine times. It is variously translated, but it basically combines two elements: relation and redemption. It refers to a close family member who steps in to defend, protect, and provide for the needy. It's a word used to describe God's past action of redeeming Israel out of Egypt, and the later prophets also used it repeatedly to describe a future redemption what God would accomplish...Let's read there and find out about what kind of Redeemer God is and what kind of Redeemer the Messiah will be...The Messiah is like Boaz. Notice Ruth's important genealogical

[5]David Murray, *Jesus on Every* Page (Nashville, TN: Thomas Nelson, 2013), 61.

postscript that further boosts the messianic momentum by tracing her descendants to King David.[6]

Would you like to know how God redeems? Look at Boaz. In what ways will the Messiah redeem? Boaz unlocks the answer for the Old Testament reader. Exodus 14 reveals God redeeming a nation through the Red Sea with power and finality. What is the personal side of God's redeeming love? Boaz cracks the code.

Using the English Standard Version, notice the use of "redeem" and "redeemer" (just in the third and fourth chapters of Ruth) and let the words leave an indelible mark on your mind and heart (emphasis added):

> He said, "Who are you?" And she answered, "I am Ruth, your servant. Spread your wings over your servant, for you are a *redeemer*." (Ruth 3:9)

> And now it is true that I am a *redeemer*. Yet there is a *redeemer* nearer than I. (Ruth 3:12)

> Remain tonight, and in the morning, if he will *redeem* you, good; let him do it. But if he is not willing to *redeem* you, then, as the Lord lives, I will redeem you. Lie down until the morning." (Ruth 3:13)

> Now Boaz had gone up to the gate and sat down there. And behold, the *redeemer*, of whom Boaz had spoken, came by. So Boaz said, "Turn aside, friend; sit down here." And he turned aside and sat down. (Ruth 4:1)

> Then he said to the *redeemer*, "Naomi, who has come back from the country of Moab, is selling the parcel of land that belonged to our relative Elimelech." (Ruth 4:3)

> "So I thought I would tell you of it and say, 'Buy it in the presence of those sitting here and in the presence of the elders of my people.' If you will *redeem* it, *redeem* it. But if you will not, tell me, that I may know, for there is no one besides you to *redeem* it, and I come after you." And he said, "I will *redeem* it." (Ruth 4:4)

---

[6]Ibid., 62–63.

Then the *redeemer* said, "I cannot *redeem* it for myself, lest I impair my own inheritance. Take my right of *redemption* yourself, for I cannot *redeem* it." (Ruth 4:6)

So when the *redeemer* said to Boaz, "Buy it for yourself," he drew off his sandal. (Ruth 4:8)

Then the women said to Naomi, "Blessed be the Lord, who has not left you this day without a *redeemer*, and may his name be renowned in Israel!" (Ruth 4:14)

Flannelgraphs might be able to illustrate the deliverance of a nation through the Red Sea, but they cannot make the connection between the brute redemption of the nation Israel and the personal touch of a kinsman-redeemer like the kind and gracious Boaz. Even more, flannel can't connect the dots and preach Jesus from Samuel's account of Boaz (we think Samuel wrote Ruth). If Boaz' act of love in marrying Ruth was magnanimous, how much more is Christ's love for His bride? "Over and above" are good terms for the loyal love of Christ and the Christ-pointing Boaz. Robert Deffinbaugh highlights the redeemer concept writing, "Boaz set aside his own self-interest (unlike the nearest kin), so that he might be a blessing to those in need."[7] Centuries later, Paul exclaimed something similar, speaking of Jesus:

In him we have redemption through his blood, the forgiveness of our trespasses, according to the riches of his grace, which he lavished upon us, in all wisdom and insight making known to us the mystery of his will, according to his purpose, which he set forth in Christ as a plan for the fullness of time, to unite all things in him, things in heaven and things on earth. (Ephesians 1:7–10)

According to Jewish law, slaves could only be freed by a relative. The eternal Son of God cloaked Himself with flesh so that He could rescue us from sin and our slavery to it. The emancipation proclamation of Genesis 3:15 ultimately is fleshed out in the incarnation of Jesus Christ, but proximately it is on display in Ruth. Boaz redeems. Boaz is not Jesus, but he preaches Him. Sometimes the most obvious displays are the hardest to discover. Ruth needed redemption and it cost Boaz something. It was deliverance by a ransom.

---

[7] Robert Deffinbaugh, "A Light in Dark Days (Ruth)," accessed from https://bible.org/seriespage/16-light-dark-days-ruth.

Who is the ultimate Ransomer? Jesus' life was the price of purchase. The refrain of Paul, Peter, and the writer of Hebrews is in unison:

> waiting for our blessed hope, the appearing of the glory of our great God and Savior Jesus Christ, who gave himself for us to redeem us from all lawlessness and to purify for himself a people for his own possession who are zealous for good works. (Titus 2:13–14)

> knowing that you were ransomed from the futile ways inherited from your forefathers, not with perishable things such as silver or gold, but with the precious blood of Christ, like that of a lamb without blemish or spot. He was foreknown before the foundation of the world but was made manifest in the last times for the sake of you who through him are believers in God, who raised him from the dead and gave him glory, so that your faith and hope are in God. (1 Peter 1:18–21)

> he entered once for all into the holy places, not by means of the blood of goats and calves but by means of his own blood, thus securing an eternal redemption. For if the blood of goats and bulls, and the sprinkling of defiled persons with the ashes of a heifer, sanctify for the purification of the flesh, how much more will the blood of Christ, who through the eternal Spirit offered himself without blemish to God, purify our conscience from dead works to serve the living God. (Hebrews 9:12–14)

As a child, cable ties scared me. The one-way tightening. Pictures of blue fingers pre-Facebook were nightmarish. Yikes. Sin is like a cable tie. It is secures itself and just keeps ratcheting tighter and tighter. But unlike a cable tie, no human can remove the choking bands of his or her own sin. Deliverance must be by power and precision. The brilliance of Christ's redemption through the ransom price of His own blood is an escape worth singing about. B.B. Warfield proclaimed,

> There is no one of the titles of Christ which is more precious to Christian hearts than "Redeemer"...Redeemer is the name specifically of the Christ of the cross. Whenever we pronounce it, the cross is placarded before our eyes

and our hearts are filled with loving remembrance not only that Christ has given us salvation, but that he paid a mighty price for it.[8]

The book of Ruth preaches redemption through a redeemer. Boaz or Christ? Yes.

Conclusion

I do not have "flannel-phobia" or any kind of real aversion to flannelgraphs. I actually enjoy them and am considering a church budget request so that I can have one around for basic story concepts. I will fill in the invisible blanks with the Bible and some Christ-centered preaching. If you do the same, make sure you follow the well-worn adage, "The Lord is my hero, I shall not want... another hero." Read, teach, and preach the Old Testament like Jesus instructed believers to proclaim it, that is, as a Christian book!

The words of R.L. Wheeler serve as a fitting conclusion to any discussion of Ruth:

> If I had the wisdom of Solomon, the patience of John, the meekness of Moses, the strength of Samson, the obedience of Abraham, the compassion of Joseph, the tears of Jeremiah, the poetic skill of David, the prophetic voice of Elijah, the courage of Daniel, the greatness of John the Baptist, the endurance and love of Paul, I would still need redemption through Christ's blood, the forgiveness of sin.[9]

---

[8] *The Princeton Theological Review*, vol. xiv, 1916, pp. 177–201. Opening Address, delivered in Miller Chapel, Princeton Theological Seminary, September 17, 1915.

[9] Edythe Draper, *Draper's Book of Quotations for the Christian World* (Wheaton: Tyndale House Publishers, Inc., 1992).

Finale:

' ' '

Where do we go from here?

' ' '

My grandmother from my father's side, was named, Erna. Technically, her first name was "Hedwig," but that did not see to bolster her popularity in the early part of the 1900s. (If I only had known that the "w" in the German, "Hedwig" was pronounced with a "v" sound. That would have saved me a lot of grief, but also oodles of laughter). So Grandma went by her middle name, Erna. Erna excelled in remedial concoctions designed for health improvements. I guess she was the wizard of home remedies. Wizard-ess? Growing up during the Depression helped people search for and find hundreds of cures. Who knows if they actually worked or just fueled a psychosomatic cure?

Three of her home remedies immediately come to mind. The first is her "medicine" for a sty. Like a sty in your eye. I have heard of "teabag compresses" applied straight to the ocular region (make sure you use separate tea bags for each eye), but a nasty piece of white bread, probably Wonder Bread, soaked in lukewarm milk? Slap that on your pupil. I bet you cannot top that poultice! I know some older folks use bread and milk for sprained ankles and joint ailments, but for your eyes? Who knew? Her second was the concoction designed to make you throw up (if you ate something poisonous). Get hot cow milk and mix it with yellow mustard. Guzzle. Upchuck. Not bad for a lady who could not afford Ipecac for emetic and expectorant purposes.

Well, the other 1930s' Depression-era cure allegedly fixed the common cold. It was noxious. It was so yucky that Mary Poppins could not ever fabricate the "Erna cure." I guarantee that Ms. Poppins never sang, "Take a spoonful of sugar and dowse it with whiskey. Force your grandson to 'eat' it." Somehow the meter and rhyme are lacking. I can still feel the burn in my throat. Cheap whiskey. Burn, baby, burn was the result. As children, we purposely tried to stop sniffling because that elixir never went down "in a most delightful way." I think I even swallowed the medicine and exclaimed, "Supercalifragilisticexpialidocious!" But I think it might have been utilized as a swear word.

In the world we currently inhabit, beware of both the sugar and the whiskey of the world's system as it seeks to obscure lies with a veil of the truth. Since boldfaced lies are easily spotted, the enemy is keen to utilize cloak-and-dagger methodologies. While lies are easily recognized, "white lies" are stealthier.

A surefire method to avoiding "evangelical white lies" is to ground yourself in a solid local church, which focuses upon verse-by-verse, Christ-centered exposition. When your pastor stresses the authorial intent of Scripture and connects every sermon to Christ's glorious redemption, you are on your way to understanding the Bible. Personal Bible reading will also help protect you.

The End?

I do not think I would be a good steward of the truths contained in this book if I concluded in a routine fashion. We need to end in a manner worthy of myth-busting, lore-shattering, and fable-splintering! See if you can spot the myths and "white lies":

- Everything your first pastor taught was true. Especially the red letter portions.

- If it is not in the King James Bible, it must be a fabrication. Thy word is truth.

- The Mayan Calendar prevents faithful stewardship past 2012, so why bother? Does it matter that it is 2016 for the Mayanistic prognosticators?

- You could never be duped by any myth. Men with clerical collars speak ex-cathedra. If you don't know what that means, simply realize Latin words are binding.

- When people say, "It isn't about the money." It. Always. Is.

- Stewardship is only relevant for the rich. Maybe the poor can garner a few lessons from it.

- Ten percent of your paycheck should be spent on buying copies of this book for your friends and church members. Think: New York Times list.

- The best advice the author can give you is to voraciously study your Bible for yourself, especially in context.

- Attend a church whose pulpit ministry is based on revealing authorial intent via verse-by-verse exposition. If the pulpit is covered with gold or is a plexi-glass tripod, beware!

- Traditions are not bad unless they contradict the Bible. Fiddler, meet Roof.

- Every hymn has biblical lyrics.

- The church is a building.

- Alcohol is, by nature, sinful.

- You are not as bad as you think you are.

- Expiation, not propitiation, is at the heart of penal substitution.

- The God of the Old Testament has evolved into the loving God of the New Testament.

- You should believe everything in this book without checking the Bible to see if it is true.

- The song, "Liar, Liar," was written in 1964 and was sung by The Castaways.

Sexual Fidelity
by Mike Abendroth

Written in NoCo style ("always biblical, always provocative, always in that order"), Sexual Fidelity is intentionally arranged with thirty pungent chapters so that the readers will study one chapter per day, with the hope of establishing consistent and biblical thinking about sexual purity. The book's purpose is to saturate the reader's mind on a daily basis, to think correctly about sex and how it relates to Christ and His church.

Originally stemming from father and son discussions about the sanctity of sex and honed in the laboratory of Men's Discipleship classes at Bethlehem Bible Church, Sexual Fidelity is perfect for men's groups, parents, students, benefiting both men and women, whether single or married.

You won't find potty-mouth discussions, but you will come face to face with God's revelation about what He created. This book answers questions like:

- Is the cycle of porn breakable?
- Can every type of sexual sin be forgiven?
- How should parents talk to their children about sex?
- Is there any hope for "dirty old men?"
- Does the Gospel relate to sexual purity and sexual sin?

Anything but moralistic, Sexual Fidelity begins and ends with the premise that the believer's union with Christ is essential for God-honoring thinking about sex. Christians will appreciate the gospel of Jesus Christ in these pages, for the gospel regularly reoccurs as the solution and motivating force to obeying God in sexual matters.

There have been times in my life when I have provided qualified endorsements of books on this subject. This time I am happy to say there are no qualifications at all. Sex is a good gift from a great God. Just make sure you handle it with care. This book will be a wonderful asset in accomplishing that crucial goal.

Danny Akin, President, Southeastern Seminary

Order at www.nocompromiseradio.com